CHORUS

ALSO BY SAUL WILLIAMS

The Dead Emcee Scrolls

, Said the Shotgun to the Head

She

The Seventh Octave

CHORUS

A LITERARY MIXTAPE

edited and arranged by

saul williams
with dufflyn lammers and
aja monet

GALLERY BOOKS MTV BOOKS

new york london toronto sydney new delhi

Gallery Books
A Division of Simon & Schuster, Inc.
1230 Avenue of the Americas
New York, NY 10020

First MTV Books/Gallery Books trade paperback edition September 2012

GALLERY BOOKS and colophon are registered trademarks of Simon & Schuster, Inc.

For information about special discounts for bulk purchases, please contact Simon & Schuster Special Sales at 1-866-506-1949 or business@simonandschuster.com.

The Simon & Schuster Speakers Bureau can bring authors to your live event. For more information or to book an event contact the Simon & Schuster Speakers Bureau at 1-866-248-3049 or visit our website at www.simonspeakers.com.

Designed by Ruth Lee-Mui

Manufactured in the United States of America

10 9 8 7 6 5 4 3 2 1

Library of Congress Cataloging-in-Publication Data is available.

ISBN 978-1-4516-4983-3
ISBN 978-1-4516-4984-0 (ebook)

a few words

Shut up and sit down. New Age be damned if the old do not heed the voice and concerns of the young. Here are the voices of many, woven into one. If each face is a book, here is a testament: the groundplan of a social network. Here are our fears, disbeliefs, visions, and wishes welded into words. Here is our love, our desires, sprung from the incessant chatterbox of our adolescence. Here is the voice of the un-dead and the un-compromised. Make no tradition of this. We have had enough.

CHORUS

moderato cantabile

1

blah blah hard-hitting
first line.

some bullshit about where I'm at.

connecting it
to something
seemingly irrelevant.

elevating a combination
of mundane thoughts
to the epic.

ask a question
to throw everyone off.

explain the past
in terms acceptable
to the present.

challenge the present
to re-consider
its coping mechanisms.

blame myself in the process.

free myself in the blame.
write about
all that I'm going to do about it.

run the risk of being condescending.

get dangerously close
to threatening.

shrug off rejection,
secretly expecting acceptance.

not saying anything about it,
as the next line
disarms with the word, 'poop,'
put in a creative context.

feel accomplished for typing,
not trying.
get tired
of thinking what comes next.

insert trademark
unconsciously.

wonder how much more
before I can stop
and go back to the luxury
of lifestyle.

prepare the rationale
that denies the distraction.

write down
whatever it takes
to not think
the word waste.

end with superiority complex
wrapped in
the cleverest thing
they done ever did
heard.

2

At the end of your ten-day meditation retreat
you got in your car
drove thirty peaceful feet
and ran over a bird,

splayed its holy guts on the pavement
like god finger-painting fuck you
across that deep breath
you were holding
the way your mother held her first born.

You, thank goodness,
were torn from the bible
the day before they burned it
for the verse about dancing to tambourines.

Once
you saw the blood of Christ on a knife
carving redwood trees into church pews.
Now every Sunday morning
you hear glaciers melting
and you see the feathers in your rearview mirror
scattering like prayers
searching for a safe place to land.

Hold me to my word
when I tell you I will leave today,
catch a bus ticket west
just to stand in the center of your highway
stopping traffic 'til every feather's answered.

I've seen too many prayers
caught in the grills of eighteen-wheelers.
And folks like us, we've got
shoulder blades that rust in the rain,
but they're still G sharp
whenever our spinal chords are tuned
to the key of redemption.

So go ahead world, pick us
to make things better.

You wanna know what the right wing never got?
We never question the existence of god.

What we question is his bulldozer
turning Palestine into a gas chamber.
What we question is the manger in Macy's
and the sweatshops our children call the North Pole.

What we question is the idea of a heaven
having gates.

Have you never stood on the end of a pier
watching the moon live up to her name?
Have you never looked in the eyes of a thief
and seen his children's hungry bellies?

Some days my heart beats so fast
my ribcage sounds like a fucking railroad track
and my breath is a train I just can't catch.

So when my friends go filling their lungs with yes,
when they're peeling off their armor
and falling like snowflakes on your holy tongue, God
collect the feathers.

We are thick skin
covering nothing but wishbones.
Break in. You'll find
notebooks full of jaw lines
we wrote to religion's clenched fist.

Yeah, we bruise easy.
But the sound of our bouncing back
is a grand canyon full of choir claps
and our five pointed stars
have always been open to the answer,
whatever it is.

Look me in the bullseye,
in the laws I broke
and the promises I didn't,
in the batteries I found when the lights went out
and the prayers I found when the brakes did too.

I've got this moment
and no idea when it will end,
but every second of this life
is scripture.

And to know that, trust me,
we don't need to be born
again.

3

i begin in a rude place praying awkwardly

my body is ugly. and a consequence of silence.

i watched myself being born

i came from crocodile mouths,
i swam thru the bronx of my mother's belly

she married those cracks in bible passages. her jesus-witch-brew
cried a liquid city between thighs and blurred
bookcases until a heartbeat broke
centuries
a noisemaker spat and bled thru his golden horn.
a poet held me down on a bed.

this is old news, all the stethoscopes have told it before

silence is scary.
i watch the singing ones and i want to move in their throats
and i want to sleep in them and wake
and not be so scared allthetime.

i don't want to talk about the kissing ones or the ones who are
smaller than their mouths who die in the middle of the street
and how small children are chastised for wanting to touch
them. who are the lullaby god's Worst . . . or the funksmell
that follows them across bridges and beneath breasts and
powders armpits with their crying.

if i could tell you i love you in a language where fear didn't
  exist
i know
i would remember the earth as a piece of my chest

4

I.

you kiss my breasts
and the blood gathers beneath my skin just to be near you.
becomes the place i bathe you
a shimmering mineral pool of diamonds and berries
oshun's honey and magnolia blossoms in bloom.
this is my dream . . .
i am a mermaid
you—
on the shore cutting watermelon
you—
feeding me
you—
rubbing oil into my hot body.
you and i
a river running through us.

II.

this was me before you—
mouth wide in the arkansas lapping the waves
that flowed from your hands.
my feet in the river
pressing blessings through rocks and mud
sending godlove anointed water to you.

i prayed for you—
through lotawatah/ and tenkiller/

and eufala/ bird creek.
deep fork.
through waters surrounded by land and air.   open sky.
through lakes and rivers who'd heard rumors
of the sight of the sea.
how the very presence of it will
drop
you
to
your
knees.

i sang your ship to me
sang the siren song that was in my belly the first time I saw your
  face
your eyes
the unbearable beauty of you.
come to me come to me come to me come to me come to me
if you had sailed away from me . . .
if you had sailed away from me
i would have died on this rock
fish falling through my fingers like sighs.

you listened to me-
  through the altamaha/ and the ohoopee/
the ogeechee.
  the flint/ocmulgee/the mighty chattahoochee.
your heart and soul swimming to me.

and now?
there is nothing else that sustains me.
sweet soft. a quick/lick from a sugared spoon.

III.

your rivers are georgia pines deeper than green.
    the liquor in a pot of collards. a smoky bone.
    the tip of your tongue in my mouth.
taste the salt of my tears.
you are macon mud rich
a frozen rock
in a hot spot.
me
breaking through to the core.

my rivers are sky and sky and sky
a little golden girl barefoot on the creek plains
arms reaching to the sky/waiting for the storm
giggling with the wind and the rain.
a perfect peach.
my outstretched hand holding for you a single drop of dew.

IV.

i am the fish that swims both ways in the river.
-they say because i'm not sure of my direction.
-i say because i wanted you to catch me.

you are the land that barely breathes.
-they say because no one had watered your garden
-you say because you were waiting for me to soak into your soil.

we are the trickle the sprinkle the geyser the gush
the creek the crawl the river the wider the ocean the awe . . .
-they say it's because opposites attract.
-we swirl in our whirlpool and laugh at the moon.

5

The moon prowls 'round
stalking at a distance.
She is a tank.

Her silent rumblings—
pass through no-man's land and
rattle our atmospheres,
the crust; blue surges,
neap and ebb,
bend outward our walls
till tiding break
the fasted lines
and we awake
to wave our sullied underclothes
up feebly
at the sky.

6

And so what that we sewed lashes on the eyelids of the moon?
dilated the sky's cervix and climbed high inside Her womb
In June, I was Oshun, and I applied the night's perfume
to the hollow of my collarbone and invited him to prune
away the shadow shroud I plied upon my loom
And so what that we ignited violet branches in my room?
shook the blooms asunder, blanched the thunder with our tune
We were titans hiding in the shrubs that line the tomb
of Babylon, playful in our nakedness we prattled
daft about how craftily we painted parallaxes
I watched him raptly humming he'd already won the battle
contemplating atoms and his brandied Adam's apple
But no matter had we splattered the canvases of Saturn
built pyramids on Pluto, or graffitied Venus caverns
He sees me no cosmic sovereign though I jewel his crown with
stars
A glitterfaced infatuate catching drinks slid down the bar
So no matter that we flattered ourselves splinters of the fracture
between the ribs of Eden and the breath of heaven's blackbirds
I am gigglethroated gloater straddling to ease his backhurts
licking ligaments and knees ripped on the edge of April's
laughter

And so what that I refuse to glue back the glass that shattered?
I am prismskinned remembrance staining days with my
refraction

7

We are all mirrors
We speak outbursts & job interview
Logos on our tongues
One movie quote away from laughter
One text message away from crying
Lips riddled with bilingual subtitles in the language
from a world we are not from
In thee business of selling the priceless
Merchants of imagination
Only good @ what we're good @
Only want 2 go where we never been without leaving our homes
Occupied without occupations
Believe in books from a time we didn't live in that break belief
into fractions
And All we are left with is long division
Down the middle
The heart is a riddle
Perspectives a weapon
Out of shape
Exercising ego till it looks like confidence
Confined 2 where our pasts have been
Late 2 a meeting with our futures
Instruments out of tune creating our own time signatures
Out of key
But open 2 becoming our own favorite songs
Dreams sound better when unexplained

Clouds look nicer when you're not flying through them
Facial features feature our parents' flaws
Microscope your every breath
Look closer
How many lives do you see?
How many lives do you live in a day?
Paralyzed by the thought of who we will be when we are not here
Is being ahead of your time choosing 2 be a non-factor in thee
now
Juggling questions like the answers are up 2 us
Gravitating 2 a place with less of it
Look at me looking at you when looking @ me
How do we look?
We ignore each other because we don't have anything left 2 say
after hello
Unsure of what beauty is anymore
We look in mirrors 4 a story we've never seen before
Ask stars questions we are the answers 2
We are flowers beautiful without ever seeing a picture of
ourselves
Watered by the moments we love ourselves
Caught in
We love we
we love us nots
What is more beautiful than we?
We are hellos we've never met
Faith without church
Fear unlearned
Life without worlds
poetry without words

8

poems about birchwood are bullshit
unless forests of mercantilists burn
tied to tree trunks, skin smoldering
trail of dental records, inheritance
in flames   motherfuckers
kicked in the nuts postulating posturing
tweed tenure track post-poetry imposters,
we want poems that dance around the ear,
machete and tech 9 pressed against the temple
poems that will kill someone / tonight—demigods
false idols, crack Donald's Hall of mirrors
no horses head genocide   just assholes
squeezing gates of definition tighter. they
never get fucked. they only give department head:)

we want poems that tie Billy Collins to a chair
and beat him. we'll see how pretty, witty and meaningless
it all is: a million stanza march ready to flood his organs
alternate multi-cult cannons shoved in his paternalism
backfire prosody until his blank eyes' black

we want poems to stop lying
in showers of middle-age heartbreak &
cancer. fucking grad students ain't noble.
poems that grab *New Yorker* subscribers
by their neckties, hang them in Morning-

side Heights, Harlem, West Wicker Park
River North, University Village like piñatas
summertime shooting galleries, gentrified
chicken shit wax-that-ass museum displays
of quaint colonialists discovering a cafe.

white poems about whiteness devils & white
powder medicine men. poems that stole everything
we own & won't surrender. 40-line reparation pathologies
to jazz writers who beat-bopped a century of plagiarism
who beat-box between line breaks, who cop language
break /ups and think they in OH! /vating

white poems / little dick slavery poems
blueprints rolled on the table in daylight
poems that cut school funds / a(f)firm
white woman ass/imilationists, dic-
tion bigots, cracker gun barrels, white poems
w/ mathematic inconsistencies, voter fraud
interest-rate hikes, red lines & red-stamped
bank loans. poems that smother children
in knock-off handbags & Nike shoes
poems starved for attention. a white poem
that destroys a white world that eats itself
rather than consumes the Other finally
a poem that will grab the king's keys & stab
fair maidens and game wardens repeatedly
the royal court bloody, shocked & clawed.

9

I'll kill your baby.
Then, I'll come for you.
Wenches awake jaw-drooped,
weltering from my machete-clipped wings.
Submerged in vinegar sweat,
clenching Christ crosses, they moon-chant:
Night Owl, Night Hag: You Can't Scare Me.
Night Owl, Night Hag: You're The Enemy!
I'm their martyr
peroxided in scripture,
now the heresy who rejected Adam's body
atop. He cleaved onto Eve
who still left him foolish. I leave men wet
with dreams of women with bird-taloned feet
taking flight greeting angels at the Sea.
Docile Marys fetter selves to rock,
dirt gardens, preferring the sting of stones
inscribing *maid* on their backs.
Their daughters invent Bloody Lillith
with lights out, terrified
my likeness will burst through their mirrors:
Who second-sexed these servants?
Dared they lie beneath men
& raise boys?
Who exiled me from their tongues?
I cut throats & uteruses

If I, who denied beneathness,
am now beneath,
why not slice open their bellies
& score their wings?

10

This a bus with wings
Flying me high above the earth
I need red clay forgiveness
I need a nina simone gun
With no bullets
Just fire
Just freedom

I bite down hard at my bottom lip
To remind myself of the pain
To feel something soft on my
Body filled with concrete, metal
And somebody else's needles.

I am a shadow of myself.
I am the after-hour party
The next stop is my stop
Any stop. Just don't stop

Keep driving bus driver
Till we touch the first
Cloud in the entrance to

Heaven.

There has to be a safe place
For women who had a yesterday
And a series of uncertain
Tomorrows.

This window is the entire
World. Maybe the earth is
Flat and square after all.

Maybe I would stop running
In circles if I just went to
The edge of this mutha fucka

And jumped.

This is better than jumping.
This is a church revival. Ooh. Baby.
They could never save me in those
Pretty places. Too much stained
Glass. I need to be able to see
Inside.

I wanna hear my God in a simple place.
The loud speaker at a drive-
through menu.

There u are. I can hear you talking to me.
I love French fries. Always have. I can
Fix a lot of things about myself. That one
I ain't changing.

Changing. What the hell is that anyway.
We all the same from the moment we are born.
Aren't we?

I'm moving, but I'm still me. I don't have a
Costume. Not for this life. I will ask God
For a new one next time around, maybe.

Change is good. Things we can't control we
Name good. Getting high is good, when u can
Control it. Check that out.

I just want to eat and sleep for a few months. Wake up
As a movie star in a different movie. And maybe more meat to
cover these bones.

This is not my movie. I had to convince myself.
So here I am, a jar full of empty promises
and letters never sent.

I couldn't hold him. I didn't know how to hold him.
Who was gonna hold me? Huh?

Why we only born with these two hands anyway. Explain that
Shit to me. Women need more than two. What if
Someone cut these off. It happens.

Or arms. They can just fall off from exhaustion.
What's up modern medicine. Help me grow some new arms!

Why can't we just grow new ones? Humans ain't so special.
Can't just heal our wounds by a touch or a kiss. That's never
  enough. We gotta take pills
to fix Our brains. We so smart, we don't know how

to think.

Without some help.

That's all I need. A little help.
A cross to bare. A bridge to cross.
I am not broken. Just tired.
Damaged slightly.

Nothing good lasts forever.
And sometimes nothing bad does either.

This is my stop. Can we land now
Bus driver?

That old bridge exists in the reflection
Of the new. Simply beautiful. I need
To sleep somewhere like that.

I need to wake up in the care of the sun.
I need to feel safe with my eyes closed.

I need to land. Like an alley cat.
I paid my fare a million times.
I am not a secret!!
I am screaming
Inside this shell.

Time can't find me here. No more
Watches. Everybody watches.

Watch me get off.
Watch me get off.
Watch me land.

I got wings
This bus got wings.
Just put this baby in drive.

And let's fly
Let's exist together
For the very first

time.

11

who told you
you
could
expose
your
wings
black girl
don't you know there is no room to evolve here
no room to resolve fears
dissolve tears
back into the earth from which you came
your name(?)
lucy(,)
loosely
considered hominoid

human

beautiful

woman

marvel at your buttocks
and legs
slim waist
and breasts

yet make child suckling illegal in public
we need no remembrance
of what we taught you to forget
of heru and
auset
jesus and
mary
forbid to teach the babies
that the messiah had a messiah
and her name was
Mama

12

Despite your small victories
you were built for digestion.

There is a fire in your chest
that will burn you in the right
direction: follow it.

Blind yourself
with anything.
It is the only way
to walk properly;
sightless stumbling over
cobblestones, molars
under your feet.

Tonight, you are
the offering.

Every step taken
is a minor rapture
for your tongue,
your nose, ears,
and hands heightened
by the surrendering

of your pupils. Walk
your heels skinless,
until your blisters
are just pads

of pulp. And then, when you collapse,
sprawled out like a starfish, you will love

with your whole body.
You will bleed the earth

a sky.

13

no one tells you
if anyone does you do not listen anyway

if you do still you do not understand
no one tells you how to be free

there is fire in your neck
ocean in your ear
there is always your fear
the words you cannot even

no one is here
when the world opens upside
down you reach toward dawn
your weight on the earth changes

some of us plant deeper
others ache to fly

14

Hot wind sprays sand in our eyes, and I know you're still angry with me.
To the west, Eden's trees sway and the cool water washes sinner skin clean.
Don't worry love, you'll be free of me soon.

Babies' blood upon my chin, sweet as pomegranate syrup. Oh, how many fetters
wrought in love and unmade by lust, were soggy-skinned and tender.
Fear not my love, you'll be clean this afternoon.

How you loved to weave the bonds and strap them to my belly. Now
the heat of your anger scorches the plain, lamenting both hunger
and its satiation. Don't worry love, you'll be free of me soon.

When our sons have a taste for their young, you'll remember me.
Attributing a lineage of sin to your sister, though I only meant to
bring you unburdened to your fate. Oh my dear one, remember this tune.

Eve waits in the shadow of a fig tree, the virgin daughter.
Her juices will still feel unclean on your fingers,
Tasting not quite right. You're impossible to please, just like your Father.

Dearly beloved, this demon's love for you was true;
Here you stand at Earth's gate, I've carried you through!
Lust and fire defeated, remand me to the dunes;
For all that I bore you, I'll be free of you soon.

15

It is fine to mourn the dead
--- but this is not that poem.

This for those we haven't lost.
This for those
who couch surf until
waves of hospitality cease cresting.

Then, they crash
on floors before
they find another place,
paddle over and pray
the tide rises high
enough to hang 10
or however many days they can.

This is for those

whose disorganization
was amusing and endearing
until it cost them college,
those for whom
"damn homie
in high school you was the man homie
the fuck happened to you?"
was written.

This is for those
who only call once
ever 5-7 months and
have the same conversation
each time,
like pop songs

— the chords might change

but the progression's the same.

It starts with

a warm greeting

and details suggesting

progress paid a visit

before the cover

of enthusiasm fades,

revealing

the only real change:

their location.

Sad nostalgia infects

their voice, reminding

of every errand and chore

and other reason to

get off the phone

right now.

This is for those
people, we all know
those people.
They were our best friends
growing up, the ones we looked up to.
Now we can hardly find
the energy for half a smile
whenever they cross our paths.
This is for those
because after so many
unsuccessful efforts,
offering help feels
like attempting to push
the boulder of Sisyphus,
it seems absurd to even try.

All that remains is hope
and hope can elect a president
but it can't save a person's life

so we write and read
poems like these,
like lighthouses and maybe
those people will find their way
back to shore.

This is for those we haven't lost
because there is a fate worse than death

and it's living to hear eulogies
for the person you could have been

16

There was no way
to say goodbye
that last day I tried.
There was thank you.
There was I love you.
There was a hand to hold
and your eyes
and the great shifting paintings
of your windows.
The ocean and the sky
and you, so tired,
everything deserting you.

Years unwinding to this;
From far away, I call,
trying to keep your voice in my ears.
Your warrior girl has pushed
your bed to the window.
Your head rests with the rising
of the sun and of the moon.
How many hearts broke
themselves, trying to hold

and keep, before she
who could stop a coal truck
with her will? She makes you soup.
The waves break over her.

I knew, this morning,
before it came.
You had gone under,
deep beneath morphine
and out with the tide.
I am here, helplessly alive
trying to find you.

You, the long, brown, gypsy boy,
trailing your ragged beauty.
You, the man,
wild-eyed and righteous,
throwing your shoes at the murderer
behind the pen. You, your shirt
splotched with my tears. You
laughing at my absurdity.
Your shout of "What are you, drunk?"
You the maker of hangover
eggs, the eyes that shared the joke,
fellow chaser of storms.
the one who loved my swagger
and knew everything behind it.

The huge moving sea
is between us.

I no longer can hold
your disappearing hand.
Your body is as earth
and stones and all
there is to offer
cannot bring one more day
of your sweet, sleepy smile.

I cry out from the sinew,
out from the agonized clutch
of my chest. My flesh
has never seemed so undeserved.
This grief is a hurricane
that passes and passes.
The eye. The storm. The eye.

I remember you,
that last afternoon
in your high, white flat.
You were unafraid. The sky
was already taking possession.
I remember you
in that seaside room
where the windows held no shore,
only the vast horizon.

17

Trace the red cord
from tread to source
to find threads
of a crushed case,
the screeching white
rib of animal
framework splintered
through a pelt still
fresh with fleas
fragments of ivory
archways snapped
tangled in viscera
of violets bruised
rouge and mangled
tubes pulsate spurts
in the midmorning
rays till the last drops
sheen in every crevice
of the road we glance
away to avoid
the scene
a deflated carcass
disappearing
on the horizon.

18

1

Broken
Pieces of bone
Skulls
And feet
Eyes and teeth
Mixed with shattered concrete
All this is rubble
Cousins
Bricks
Steel beams
Sister
Glass, mother
Tears, blood
Brother
Babies
        Buried under all that unyielding
        Unforgiving rubble

When the dump trucks
Come to scoop up
Toes and clothes
Papers and arms
Who will take the time
To peel

Flesh off the
Cracked wood boards
Separate what was once alive
From the plastic

But sometimes in the
Rubble there is life

2

From
Under the concrete
A rescue dog hears a heartbeat
Life
Barks to alert
Dog and rescuers
Find
Warm-blooded person
Heart still beating
Pumping blood
So subtle
Buried in all that rubble
Yet this dog
Hears
There are no
Buried secrets

They
Know compassion
As they tread carefully
Walk over and through

Mountains of
Broken
Unstable
Rubble
To find life

3

8 days
Under rubble
Entombed
Only able to roll
A few inches
Wiggle your toes
Only able to pray
Psalms blocks out the panic thoughts
And claustrophobia

As earth shattering
Aftershocks
Threaten, threaten
To rain death on you
But the rumbles are the
Machines
Chomping through
Concrete
Wires
Broken glass
They find you
Under 10 stories of concrete
You were at work when
The earthquake hit

Your husband gives you a bit of water
Poured through a small hole
You see light for the first time in over a week
That night
Dusty rescuers
Pass your stretcher
Carefully
Hand to hand
Over the hills of broken brick
You are one of the last ones found
Alive
Your husband would not give up
Stupid reporter at the scene
Shoves a microphone into your face
Asks you if you knew you would survive
"Of course, why not?!" You say in perfect English
And then to the amazement of all
You start to sing!

An IV in your arm as you carefully
Get into your car
Your grateful husband
Drives you all away so
You can see for yourself
What has happened to your island

After two weeks
An 85-year-old woman is found
Under the rubble of a church
She is frail but alive
Stained-glass windows not shattered

And then another miracle
Under a house
A skeletal six-year-old boy
Is found
He is smiling!
His face dusty
He takes it all in
His arms are open wide
Everyone at the scene cheers
He cheers
He is passed to his crying father
Who never gave up

19

in spirit scrapping seafloor merriment
i arrive wild with banshee reverie
seeking beyond
broken securities coveting access to my body
beyond
salvaged excrement
and fingers groping for self in mirrors of me

i stand in spirit ruling she body
shipping unseen
carrying burnt and ashen fears ogling to nest
wearing shards of smiles shattered yesterday

so flowers reach
i arrive standing here

spitting from bone black bones
chamber of solar symphonies
hunting flesh's grief
i tell no tales
i tell knowings of wreckage and gold
so sing me, sing me
pursing dawn's reverie

in spirit mourning exhumed seepage
i stand keeping space for dreams undealt release
and seek beyond
secluded safety
where communal sutures are necessity
when child is a dead field
none wants to turn nor cultivate
for fear incapability and that she won't harvest

i arrive rooted resilient
spiriting heart's burst against rooting timbers' sway
where presence barnacles low tides
surviving to sound of her sea calls
in response she clings

a chamber of solar symphonies and bone black bones
hunting flesh's grief
i tell no tales
i tell knowings of wreckage and gold
so sing me, sing me tilling dawn's reverie

in spirit sucking sweet of bees, i stand predisposition
breaking decay, drafting nectar from my skin
and momentum of wind where ancestors keep
seeking beyond
padded throats hoping for something without claiming
what do i call her
whatever i name

here, summoning spirit of undoing
a past pattern mistress reading feelings for belief
i shine existence with an unbound rag
and seek beyond
suicide's repetitive plight

hunting flesh's grief from bone black bones
a chamber of solar symphonies
i tell no tales
i tell knowings of wreckage and gold
so sing me, sing me bringing dawn's reverie

in spirit feeding fury, i arrive hidden
a panther
carving hymns of being and light
seeking beyond
shame housing secrets silently knotted in plastic
and stuffed in pipes of ovaries
growing beyond surgical cuttings
as above so i below
i pray to woman i know

in spirit tossing change
elevating broken hyperboles
misnamed conformities
seeking beyond
kneeling or prostrate
opening keys and shifting biology
i arrive here, standing

spitting from bone black bones
a chamber of solar symphonies
hunting flesh's grief
i tell no tales
i tell knowings of wreckage and gold
so sing me, sing me
i am dawn's reverie

20

They appear in the empty morning
thin blue whips, branching veins in their wrists,
the sweat and blood of Jesus on their tongues.

Suddenly everything is so comforting:

lakes frozen to the bottom,
a forest cathedral,

a trembling voice that sings.

21

Frozen pop canticles,
written in wormwood tomes,
measured on moral metronome,
played by the dollhouse quartet;

Little maiden blue, burqa blessed,
she holds monstrous stories told
in the spaces of her lyre; infantile,
how her voice is muffled by the cloth

Somnambulist siren, she wonders
whether the screams or the carapace,
crunching shell splintering,
count as musique concrete

Cordial contessa, she sings blessedly
of cinematic corpses laid on silver platters
and how the cracked light reflects guilt
on the soles left by the entrance.

Salome, come twirl in furs from Venus,
complete this revolution of love,
take a bullet from erotic submersibles
as they come up and over your plaid skirt

22

I cry every time I watch the scene where you burst
through the church doors
Singing louder than the choir hired to replace you,
Hummingbird.
As if it were that easy to erase you like blackboards after school
You left permanent fingerprints on your father's heartbeat
The day you reached through your mother's insides
and had to be pulled out arms first
What a peculiar melody you are
often mimicked but not quite duplicated
Gospel nursed you on her tit
But the gossip of church folk taste worse
than that of spoiled milk
Collection plates could never buy you the sequin gowns worn by
Billie and Ella
So with the passing of each season you grew salty
borrowing the sharp tongues of
neighbors to butcher your
name Sugar
forever to be known as Shug
The beckon of Big cities never reminded you of your surname,
called you whatever you
saw fit
Detroit, Chicago, and New York found your southern
hospitality charming.
A foreigner amongst family when your flesh tones

mirror a crowded room
The first time you heard yourself on wax you were a puddle
on the recording room floor
The first person you rang, your father
When the butterflies escaped your throat the dial tone swatted
them away
A Daddy's girl never fully recovers from heartbreak
So you sing the Blues
Bare yourself naked every time you step foot onstage
Belting each note from your abdomen in hopes of luring back
the winged creatures that
once belonged to you.
You've never been monogamous in your adult life teetering back
and forth between Jim,
Jack and Jameson
Some might say you have a problem, call it daddy issues
But their words fall flat.
They are out of tune with your nature
How sad it is
To be revered by everyone except those your heart
bleeds for the most
Funny how you taught Ms. Celie every lesson you refused to
learn
Forgiveness is a gift not forced but earned
One day,
a righteous indignation will rise up in you
and past-life yous will fill your shoes and walk down familiar
roads un-traveled
the ancestor's spirits will cry out a Negro Spiritual that lines
your uterus with rebellion

your guardian angel will deflect the darts
of those whose business this is none of
and when you walk down the center isle with no groom in sight
staring at eyes that blinked
you into existence
Speak the peace that has finally returned to your countryside
Wrap the branches of your fig tree around that which gave you
breath
and know, that you are finally
Home

23

I was born into a Disney menagerie with not a single goal.

It is 1967 anybody with an amp could have an ambitious
hallucination.

When I wake from the cell of my dressing room, I feel the bird's
flight
in my body. The wing pang, lifting heave, locating itself above
my slumped shoulders and shoveling vines with my single voice.

It's just a voice, brunette with bangs, floating, dirigible,
ready to explode
but can't. So I snatch a pair of drumsticks and love
their suspicious feel
in my hands. Secretly, I want to smash glass.

I hate the color of an obedient deed so why do I sing its octave?

Notes that open in compassion, ribcage propped apart. My heart
lodged too close to my ribs. I'm a tree-limb steady in a high ball
generation of acid and Joplin slang.

From the surface of a mirror, my body emits hues
of yellowish orange. I hear the click of distasteful tongues
disturb my perfect silence. The motion of twirled knitting sticks
and the way yarn licks the air as it snarls towards me.

The crocheted mass, an exquisite dangle from my lap.
That's the music that's mine. I don't want sex, just synchronicity.

There is a stadium grace when I sing. Sand and the streets
breathe the same cacophony of sing-song jangle and station
wagons.

I'm able to fill a cavity
with a 4/4 drum riff wedded
with the throat call of longing.

The camera adds 30 pounds. But pounds of what?

30 pounds of silverware
30 pounds of fan mail
30 pounds of stroganoff

My heart beats so fast I enter slumber. I hear
the winged timpani in my chest. I enter a sleep . . . A black note
floods the swollen roof of my mouth, an empty beehive home,
a Los Angeles suburb . . .

If only the skeleton of a girl like the white key of a withering
piano
could sing. An ambulance siren . . . that bird's contralto.

My mother picks me up. Karen, I'm sorry . . .
The clock of attachment stops.

24

Having been a child-star actress is a double-edged dildo.
(Insert a metaphor about getting fucked here.)

No one should have to look back to see
the bright future ahead of them. The future holds

then pushes you away.
So I'm done

trying to muzzle the sterilized bevel of a best friend.
I'm gonna tie those pamphlets for cures around this needle
and wave the white flag.

I just want to lean into the duct tape
this vial is holding up to my mouth.
Cut creativity's circulation off.
Get some rubber nooses together and gang-bang my arm.

Growth has outgrown me.
I'd rather not be a word
associated with weeds and dicks.

I'd rather spend all that future brightness
looking up La Brea's sparkling skirt at dawn.

Hitchhiking up that boulevard's famous slit,
catching a ride with some opiates and trading spit.

I've heard Junk is starring in Scorsese's next movie.
This syringe knows people.

Forget my Mother and Father in all this.
They are a language that died on an ancient tongue.

I'm going solo now. I'm going to floss my teeth
with the pubic hair of the Hollywood night air,
memorize my lines before I snort them.

I want to know what it feels like
to die in the arms of missing limbs.

To fade to black,
then fade through that.

To get on my knees and crawl
on all fours into character.

To end an act in my own skin,
covered in someone else's skeleton.

25

I used to live with a bottle of whisky and my panties crumpled on the floor of some man's hard wood. That is not to say that I was always drunk or that he was just a man and not Billy, Jim, or Ben, sometimes Kathy, Mia, or Beth when I was twenty.

I used to remind myself that I was living, a modern goblet cradled in my palm like messiah-made Vermouth; Or, as if the glass were a breast waiting to feed me.

Shuffling to the bathroom late at night, I thought the lights looked like moons in the vanity mirror, an orchard of dense halos protected by metal framing that I wanted to touch but could not reach. What a paradise I thought I was making. What a trick, to hide and then forget that I was hiding.

26

It sounded made up. And after
five hours of neuropsychological
testing, of being faced with beads
I could not arrange on wooden posts,
of Stroop tests, of blocks I couldn't
position in the patterns they asked,
of recalling lists of words I recited
but did not properly organize into
categories to help me remember them--
I did not want some made up diagnosis.

I wanted drugs. I wanted a pill
I could take that would provide
concentration, motivation,
organization and every other "ation"
I needed and never had. But I only
got one-- an explanation.
For my whole life. A fucked up
looking glass to recolor history--

the reason I have no mental filter,
why I only like music for the lyrics
not the actual melodies, why
I can't find my way out of a paper bag,
the cause of my bad handwriting
and hatred for anything math-related,

the basis for my fear of exercise
and team sports, the root of why I don't
get art or philosophy or why I got
enraged every Sunday when my ex
wanted to do puzzles or play Scrabble.

But when you're 30 and you learn
your white matter doesn't function
properly and that's why you keep
getting fired from bullshit jobs,
why you can't sustain relationships,
keep friends, why you can't ever
keep your mouth shut, why you
insist on always telling the truth
even when you're becoming
your rude, crazy grandmother
who yells, *"he's too old for her,*
she can do better," in the middle
of your cousin's wedding ceremony--

it's not any kind of comfort. It doesn't
turn failures away. It just reminds
you that you never had a choice.
It proves that a malfunction in the right
hemisphere controlled personality,
formed what you could and couldn't do,
and ensured that you take everything,
even the diagnosis, the wrong way.

27

I've bought the bloody myth
swallowed that sucker
hairy legs and all
crawled careless into bed with a fantasy
and now I'm hopping antsy with expectation

having drawn these crooked lines
in what looked to me like sand
my uncertain frame stands
hooked
on what I have been promised by the TV
by that saccharine ache Anita Baker
moans from a mass-produced CD

The game of happily ever after in love
is a cruel farce
the lonely wish of a gullible asshole
who somebody done told
a whole lot of silly lies to
love is nothing
but the by-product of a teenager
wagering hormonal changes
against the smell of his own diluted sperm
spilling innocent into his awkward palm

Love is the alms
given to the poor to divert

focus from the difference
between the shacks that teachers live in
in Brooklyn
and the mansions that senators fuck young interns
in Washington DC

I am just about ready to give up
on man/woman
dog and tree
the whole romantic tic is hogwash

The idiots
who look like they might still be in love
have only been together
for three weeks
and those lucky enough to have lasted more than a year
are rapidly shifting gears
towards chopping the shared
now dysfunctional cat
in two equal parts
so they can cart the rest of their shit
to the new apartment
they cannot afford by themselves

I am tired of searching for Ms. Right
always something wrong
with the one girl who likes me
too smart/too skinny
too much of a ninny
too short/too tall

too-much-of-a-mall-girl for my liking
too free/too taken/too I'm sorry I was mistaken
in my initial assessment of your sexuality
          sometimes
I think I hang my hat too high
for my own arms to reach
which brings me back
to my original hypothesis
of love being somewhat like the perfect orgasm
          the trip there
is infinitely better than the letdown
of having already experienced it

          After the first
actualization of intercourse
there's no up to go from there
what is one to do with the sticky wet
of saliva
and vaginal fluid
and sweat
not drying fast enough
in the center of a lumpy futon
you are desperately trying to fall asleep in

Love
as I have understood it
is primarily disappointment
and hard work and very little return
so now I'm canvassing for volunteers
to go tar the cupid who conjured

the stupid concept
feather the fucker and leave the body to burn

28

we are the cunt|fused. hour vaginas tighten to virginity over and over. each time. ti|me up, in|to what dicks think|are entrances to a 4th dimension. excuse me! call me miss mister; pussy, this pen|is – my own.
eye ink. jizm.
sum do knot no how two take me? i nor eye can be red. sea me wave hy|men to sea|men, swim backward thru (hys)teria and untangle o|varies: oh my, oh my god, oh my God|damn, She is not a He, but hem is.

scissors in hand, they run up on me. cut in front of me|in me|from behind. *when one's perception is globalized to one|size fits all, sodomy ensues*; belief systems blare in bass. traditions tweet on tips of thwarted tongues – spoke|in sounds the unconscious can't turn down. they peddle hidden ace under sleeve. trick-deal drawn from unzipped pants. rod and staff got balls|banging loud beats against thighs. the eyes. the eyes, yes! *unravel.*
bend for|ward, grab toes, brace|your psyche. there is no room for sanity in the inn. dawn of (r)age – New|Or|Eve's could never trust A|dam. women know, the patriarchal world been yelling since birth – "FEE|MA; you can't afford liberty, just|ice. we will send prayers instead of help|better yet, we will send our

summer son. all liquids evaporate to heaven!" melt. submit. be pass(I've) heard them say|in corridors of cocked legs|for cuntrol of categorization. cauterization? eye burn and can only re| member – lobotomies sever things.

i am too|spirited. Berdache. native. eye nor i, need make-up. keep your shadow, it saddens. to hell with a|Mary|K|K|K's ass. Amerikkkaz mine too. squeezed this whole land through head cock-tip. cocked head as drill bit, and dug out through the universe's nappy dugout. I can b/earth a baby. male? female? trans|rendered.
you've come to me before, in fact, with these same late-term papers on fiction: phrenology, eugenics! how many times must i bash skull, break bone and dismember ignorance? abort you overboard a slave ship? drown you in an Atlantic vision? give in|sight to your blind-spot; four-eye can reflect on degrees of dualities – keep dividing me like you do, and I'll compound, cell your memory away to c|ancers of questions never thought to be asked. dislodge you from the dis|ease of forgetfulness.
a rainbow can comprehend the spectrum of sex, its combination of shades, potentiality. eye bet all the colors of my life.
put this in blood red on my wombstone; "He grew bigger, longer and harder than our soft, limp understanding could withstand – She opened a wet canal that swallowed us stillborn."
you are dead in me|my intuition: a bellyful of beasts.

29

Not that there's anything wrong with that is the same chickenshit side step as *no disrespect intended* or *I swear not to come in your mouth,* no homo.

Hip hop just has the balls to drop
onto the palm of the modern lexicon, no homo.

At some point every man learns you
gotta be the biggest dick in the room to not get fucked, no homo.

Gentlemen, you cannot let a sound run over your lips
that does affirm the rock hard nature of your identity, no homo.

Erect a panopticon in your throat
as if the world had a flashlight up your ass, no homo.

I am the last person to tell you
that it is safe in a man's skin, no homo.

30

his lighter drowns in the river so we practice kissing
instead of smoking. he talks as if

he is starving but i'm not sure what he's starving for,
food or words, water or my touch. i eat meat
with every meal, he says,
& i say, i'm vegetarian. he laughs.
he understands the need to move, the way i spit
on anxiety by walking until 3 in the morning,
when the full sky & my heartbeat are finally calm,
even if he doesn't understand my gender
or the tiny hairs on my chin & between my eyebrows.

the moon is bright the way my sister looked
after she started taking meds, glowing,
her eyes don't jitter anymore, & they don't cry either. he takes off
all his clothes, trips on the ankles of his pants,
& i almost laugh at his cock, not because the last time i touched one
my hair was down to my waist & my name belonged to a girl,
but because of how smooth it is compared to the wet sand
clumping between my toes. i say
i hope you know this makes you a fag. he says nothing
& keeps kissing my neck.
there are bubbles of hard cider in our stomachs.

flat chests confuse me. i am looking
for something to cup & hold on to with my hands but his body
is like the river & it is slipping away
through my fingers.
i didn't sleep very well last night.
he is drunk on my cum & in the morning

he will forget that i am a boi.
tomorrow i will sigh & my friend will ask,
why are you having trouble sleeping?
& i will shrug as if my shoulders are mountains
& say i don't know & start talking about the weather.

it feels so strange to fuck someone but never hold their hand.
i can hold his hand with my breasts or my cunt
but not with my fingers.
fingers woven together are too fragile & intimate.
fucking is easy. fucking is easy?

i pick at my skin when i am anxious.

31

You call me a fruit,
and I agree,
say

a fruit is ripe,
promising seeds,
bursting with juice.

You call me a fruit,
as though a vegetable

and I recite a litany
of fresh attributes:

a fruit is rich,
remembers its roots,
nourishes, quenches,
makes a display of any table.

I say,
I am the apple
that announces the gravity
of a given situation;
I am the pomegranate
whose gemstones teach
of the burden of possession;
I am the fig
our ancestors couldn't resist.

You call me a fruit
and I agree:
soft, round and sweet.
I dare you to peel back my layers,
take a look at my pips.
Full as a melon,
sharp as a lime,
come over here
and bite me.

32

My mother always asks if I'm eating well.
I don't worry her. I say
work late, soup for dinner, normal.
I tell her you're visiting and she asks
about the soup.

Sex is the unsaid thing, lone animal against the wall.
A silence passed down like heirlooms and knotted-up gold
chains.
Valuable, I wasn't made from lust, but from necessity.
A secret: the place between my mother's legs
where absence bred and clung
to the hairs on me as I descended.

What do you tell a woman who defines passion by security?
How do I dare measure against her life, fingers full of water,
flour-creased, a child on her hip when she stood before
the man she loved and said choose,
and he chose.

Can I show her the bowl of fruit on my floor where you sit
naked and hungry, pear juice dripping down your chin
and puddling in my own mouth?
Or ask if she has ever followed salt sweet lines
down her back with a lover's tongue?
Can I give her the handful of cherries, thick-fleshed,

like the first moment I tasted my own sex?
Imagine the smell of that kitchen; my mother
sucking pits like small wet songs on her dry tongue.

Leek rounds, rainbow chard, coriander, broth
slow-cooked, I don't mention the room
in the house of me where you live,
desire and devastation sleeping curled
together like dogs at the doorway.

We came from each other, and then we began to eat
from separate plates, elbows off
the table. She gives me her borsht recipe
without measurements,
says: do it to taste,
and I do

33

i am not beautiful
i am an elegant beast
a well-mannered monster
a charming barbarian
that will pillage your heart
with language
so lavishly violent
that you will curse me for coming

yet curse me for going
your crying and your moaning
will share the same sound

i am the storm
that will make your sunny days unbearable
but when the clouds begin to hug and swell
and push black kisses into each other
when the white and airy
becomes dark and full
you will know im in the mouth of the horizon
and she will breathe me thundering across your heaven

all good reason
says seek shelter
but you will invariably find yourself
running into a open field
the wind
shooting under your skirt
a furious sky in your hair
goosebumps on your thighs
your mouth open to catch the rain
that smacks your face
your tear ing eyes
towards heaven
waiting for me to send down
my most gorgeous disaster
my most frightening lovely
for which you have spent your sunny days supplicating
woe to you, God has answered your prayer

34

"We need a doctor in the ICU, description elderly couple, 1
suffering from a shivering equinox
The other bad case of eclipse"

Momma "We didn't hang their ghost out long enough to dry"
washboard, clothes line
It's always hard wringing the bones out of a spirit

Some days, I fold my throat; pack it in the truck of a black
hearse cramped
Middle passage cruise liner, hopscotch down
Route 81, countryside hums like midnight, the air thick with
the history of me
Here I'm all white picket fence and picket sign

"Check their vitals"

My great-grandparents used to bathe in onyx, bore last names
delicate as cotton
"Garner" with an ER like sirens, gurneys or an
Eerie house sculpted from the pulse of one womb

The smell of a praying skillet playing jacks with a pot of grits
Back burner like welts, Church on Sunday morning, in a town
That tastes like nooses, winters fever porch swing backyard
hammock

Fist full of rice, jumped the broom, segregated blood waiting on the other side

"Let's put him over here, lift"
"Boy this contraption can't hold me long, what's my superhero name iron lung"
Marlboro lights and silence is all I know of my great grandfather
Worked the coal mines, called him big O for Otis, godly hands, grip
Like a bear trap shake Christ out of you,
Earthly man, never able to crack the husk of him
Crucified footprints, dirt roads burning U-Hauls
The clan moved in next door

"We're going to have to run more tests"
"Come rub gram grams feet, massage a few decades from my steps"
My great-grandmother's name was Esther
All apron and foxhound had a bite like boycott, smiled like pistol whips
2 green thumbs patch of land, her eyes two dilating ashtrays
Ribcage furnished like a western salon, bar fight laughter
Protest the moonshine, this is a sit-in

"Not to be the bearer of bad news, but we found something, no cause for alarm with treatment
You can see 6 more months"

I'm a shade of flatline
(cough)
"Don't smoke cigarettes, son "
Otis died crying crickets in his chest, crooked cops place a
handcuff
Over a heartbeat this is what you call cardiac arrest
Cells were never meant to split this way

*"I know this is hard, one by one you can go in and say your last
words"*

Poppa, hold me in your arms like a rigid mountain peak
"Shhhhh *don't tear, boy, I've been breathing like a steel mill all my
days, 'bout time I retire"*
Momma, don't leave, "Child, watch my crops, scare the Jim
crows"
see their souls rising; I take my palms to try shoving their
childhoods back into their bones

This is my defibrillator to the sky all that
Thunder clap!!
"No more bullets on hotel balconies
No fire hose baptisms
"They're not responding"
Pink ribbons, crumbling Saint Jude, heart-shaped obituaries
"I told you about my Jesus
Look heaven, freedom's waltzing across that labyrinth dance
floor

Million cloud March boots laced, silver lining stride to
redemption"
"Baby we'll see you on the other side of the colored line"

I turn to the doctor and ask him when will we have a cure for
this?

35

Not all errors are mistakes
Brutal images often evoke emotion but
offer no hope against this harsh landscape

Let us open wide the doors less fortunate
so that the heavy wind, rain and snow can rush in and
save us from the black clouds lurking over the blood red
horizon

Old incandescent lightbulbs flicker in dimly lit corridors
Let's listen to the tragically beautiful silence of the morning
after
There is no escape from the time and place where fiction occurs

36

Of the sunken barge in the water where life has taken root,
we know the moral.

We know where there is waste something can be profited.
We know for nature there is no waste.

Only opportunity. That is the charge you granted us,
early in the garden, before we ducked behind the elephant ear

to hide our nakedness. That was the first charge, at least.
The second: that we'd never forget.

We know that all we realize is derivative of your love.
That everything we know will not eliminate what we don't:

why parade this beauty in our faces? Why make desirable
the bones of the men who must have embraced

the night the barge slipped under? Forgive me, Father.
I am human. That means I have an ego.

That means I can't find solace in the tree that now commands
this ship, the branches stretched and twisted as your love,

although they also, like the bones,
make me choke.

37

What do you want me to say,
that I like the idea of being an animist, trees my
preferred object of worship? Not once has any tree
ever told me a thing let alone scooped me up and saved me
from the impending flood or an army of orcs surging
from the bowels of earth, sorry, Gaia, ok, Yemaja,
-yeah, yeah, The Ocean, let me finish-

I *have* listened carefully . . . once I climbed a six-story-high Maple to listen.
Just when I felt I was making some headway a drunk childhood friend
(we were friends since we were children and then adolescents experimenting
with everything from heights, to alcohol to God, just like you want to
instead of normal flirting) climbed one branch above me to see what I was up to.
The last branch actually, which snapped under her light, perfect athletic young body.
She fell six stories, landing on her back conscious enough to know instantly
she was paralyzed and would never ski again. No, that by no means broke her
faith, nor mine, but I highly doubt swapping notes on spiritual practices
is her preferred method of flirting. She is still devoted to sports.

I have not had visions when holding crouching dog for too long
or is it arching crane?
I have done neither, but one time I went to Havana with a
person much like yourself.
We got a reading from a santero, he gave us beads and a deity
each, the beads were so heavy
we had to take the D Train to Brighton Beach and throw them
into the sea.

I'm short of breath in saunas so I have never done a sweat lodge
but three of my four
deadliest car crashes happened in Vermont where there are
many non-Native American
sweat lodges
and after emerging miraculously unscathed from the gnarled
remains of 3 out of 4 accidents
(once it was snowing) the sky was profoundly clear and blue,
yeah like a door,
maybe a window, not sure.

Sure I've had a poem just *'come to me as if I were a mere vessel,'*
but not for
a long time and even those needed editing. Nothing sticks a
thorn in my crown
more than a poet fishing to get laid with some spiritual mumbo-
jumbo all prostrate
in a room full of guppies. You are correct, the gods' ability to
arouse is profound and
not inappropriate but it can be awkward, like in '85 when I
wanted to convert to Catholicism

in Apizaco Mexico because I was obsessed with the glow-in-the-dark crucifixes
sold outside the church, I wanted to buy as many as I could to sell to
Madonna fans in Boston but felt it would only be appropriate to convert first.
As I toyed with the idea, the idea grew until I could feel generations of Aztecs
pass through me when an old woman brushed my shoulder after prayer. Finally
one evening, after feeling embarrassed about buying yet one more glow-cross
from the same guy five days in a row, I stuffed it in my pants, it began to glow, I felt it,
my abdomen abuzz, my first look at a Victoria's Secret catalog, ten, alone in the bath.

For all I know God is in lunch, during Ramadan we chose God over lunch for a month.
At sixteen I walked into La Grande Mosquée and announced I wanted to convert to
Islam.
They asked me to say *Allah ila haa Mohammedan rasulullah,* so I did.
They said, *There ya go, you're a moslem.* Yes, it felt anti-climactic even in French.
Then again, celebrating Eid a year later with two thousand other moslems
in the foothills of the Himalayas in un-self-conscious synchronicity was proof

that Allah passes through all of us, with each transfer of spirit,
unknown energies
are more palpable. Many times that year I had out-of-body
experiences
to the point where I could see myself in context and realized I
looked
as post-colonial as the Aussie hippy in Haridwar, saffron robes,
beads
and bald head tonguing down his girl in front of Maya Devi
Temple.

I will tell you this, one week after my brother died I saw
something in the sky
(no, I won't tell you what it was) that affirmed my belief that
everything,
every faith, myth, superstition, miracle, rumor, conspiracy, cult,
self-help program,
everything, all of it is true.

38

Truth: I have never apologized for my own skin before,

for the way Newark bends me like sunrise gleaming through bus
windows

or the way I let myself go like doves at the matrimony of fate
and free will.

Tell me this is the way things fall apart.

Truth: My ex-significant lover walked out of Buddy Wakefield's feature last night on the
premise that God lives in North Carolina between the eye of a needle and the thread
weaving Aesop's fables together. He claims to have a keen ability to detect heresy and,
apparently, lynch mobs don't need rope or melanin before.

Lie: I am to blame.

Lie: A legacy of shame on the underbelly of a nation can be remedied
with
handshakes and convenient silence.

Truth: There are times when I am insecure in my humanity,
in the way my
body contorts and bleeds to keep this universe in balance.

Truth: Prejudice is the only way we've learned to box our own shadows,
saints whose
halos are one photon short of revealing themselves.

Truth: God could exist in the air,
blowing string-theory daffodils into the
nothingness without a care.
Would our trespasses be any less holy?

Dare-
tell me what your God looks like
sitting on a crumbling mountain of misdeeds
and
family trees bending in the wind.

Tell me how he learned to hate his own shadow,
how he taught his spitting images to split and
splinter
until we became the crosses that broke his spine.

Tell me how hate became dogma,
how love became an international distress signal.

Truth? God is a cutter.

She parades slash marks around Paradise
and plays with asps in her spare time;
call her Cleopatra with a mortal complex.

On her last bad day,
she lucid dreamt the Matrix and called it "Earth"
because "Gaea" sounded too easy to fall in love with.

She is in love with energy.
(She only gave humans sex organs because she confused us with
the trees.)

Truth: God is a woman with Body Dysmorphic Disorder,
but she can come back if we let her-
stop superimposing our rough drafts of God

onto an unsuspecting deity
because she is running out of room on her arms
to carve an identity from.

Still workshopping the theory of everything
being birthed in her belly,
she hasn't gotten to existence yet.

Save sexuality for second grade,

for she is just learning to spell her name
in kindergarten calligraphy,
and I guarantee it looks nothing like
Jesus or Buddha or Allah,

like Krishna or Moses.

It looks like big-bang theories
collapsing under the weight of change,
like a little boy finger-painting forever with a smile on his face

and it sounds, suspiciously, like home.

39

You are the sweat on the brow of a mother
in her thirteenth hour of labor.

You are the fickle fingers of a child grazing
a splintery fence midday.
You are a sixteen-syllable sentence uttered
by a woman with beautiful lips.
You are the thousands of end-of-the-world
kisses in constant exchange at each
terminal.
You speak and rain falls upward.
You blink and butterflies dissolve.
There are shells of people out there trying,
each day, to become an atom in the vast
dance of your movements,
to seek the mode in the range of your
emotions.
You are bottled nebulae with a cork
that is waiting to pop
You are lunar flora: prickly pear cacti which
fill craters steeping in a celestial marinade
hailing from the Horsehead.
And should you stand beneath the sun for too
long, the land which surrounds you
would recede into the dark recesses
from whence it came,
and the soft luminescence of your eyes
would suffice to lead your way.

40

We learn in grade school,
that there is a finite amount
of matter on Earth. All that will ever
be on this planet, already is.
And there will never be any less.

It's a hard concept to accept at first.
Because every last bit
of my grandmother's body
seems to be gone. But in fact,
science says, even if you cremate
the arms and legs and ribcage
of the person you loved,
every molecule is still here,
it's just that all the space
between the bones and the blood
is now eliminated, and so,
someone that used to take up
a whole bed, now, fits into a shoebox.

And my best friend's daughter,
seemed to just start growing
inside her, as if she came from
nowhere and nothing,
but in fact, she is actually,
all the hamburgers

that her mother ate
for nine months
transformed into fingers and toes
and green eyeballs and golden curls.

And the only exception at all,
the only way for more matter
to arrive on earth is if meteors
or some other astronomical objects
unexpectedly glide our way
to land on one of our islands
or in one of our seas
and that's what I think
I want to liken Love to,
at least for the metaphorical
purpose of this poem.

Because when it arrives, it does so
with an other-worldly crash
into the continents that are
our chests. And it is so strange,
so new, that I cannot believe
it was here all along, disguising itself
as some other thing.

I know, science says, Love is not matter,
but most days, it feels heavier than rocks.
And what I want to know
is where it goes when you
feel certain that you cannot
find it anymore.

There are ex-wives all over
the world, who at one point,
promised everything they ever knew
to their husbands,
allowed children
that were made of half of him
to swim inside her,
and drink from her,
and she thought he was a miracle,
better than any other answered prayer,
and then he destroyed her somehow.
Somewhere along the way
he forgot how extraordinary she was,
stopped seeing the certainly amazing
parts of her, and now
she hates him with a fever
that could cook a stew.

But where did all that Love go?
Where does it sit now, though perhaps
quiet, changed, but still with the same
number of atoms and molecules,
once as big as a mountain, now as small
as a seed—but it has to be here
somewhere, right?

I myself, have Loved in a Large way.
Love that was the size of an army
of dinosaurs, and now, I feel nothing
for that over-and-done Love.

I almost, cannot even remember
that Love, I have to read old poems
and inscriptions to find proof that it
ever was. But it has to be here
somewhere, right?

Maybe I will find it
under the rug, or swept
into a corner that I never visit,
or inside an old compact.
I suppose I may not even recognize it
when I do. Perhaps it is just
a spoonful of glitter now, and when
I come across it I will think it is
some eye-shadow that I forgot I bought.
I will maybe just shake my head
and wonder why I ever thought
that it would look good on me.

I Love in a Large way, right now.
And if I wake up in the middle
of the night, and look quietly
at the Love that sleeps beside me,
I cannot ever imagine
it leaving this planet for anything.
I am certain, despite what science says,
that Love is matter, that it will
never go away, and never get less.
I am also certain,
that it was not here all along,

and instead, it came dressed in flame
from outer space.

41

I fasten my mouth around yours like a plummet
from the bow of a sinking ship. Suck the red wine
from your breath until it hurts, until good memory
rises above us like God-ash and nothing is real
but your tongue, your coiled breath banging
the rusty screen door of my throat like a moan
that breaks free and dances across the dark.

The sticky shiner mooned around my eye socket
like a rain cloud waters at the touch, you pull my t-shirt
delicate as knifepoint up and over my head. It stings
where his pinky knuckle carved out a chunk
in my lip like a wood splitter. I am a hazard tank of bruise
and shame; you are a prayer that remembers how to listen.
The coin-edge crest in the crook of my nose
where that lonely bastard's ring trucked into my skull
beneath that streetlight is still open and pink,
unstitched cartilage cursing at the air like an armless demon –
you place your lips on every part of me that has retreated
to a corner I never thought I'd find, soft and new,
whisper the names of each wildfire hue
beginning to eggplant swell and settle into a tornado

around my eye. *I love you,* harder than ever
and am overflowing with words I do not have.
Again. We are naked as morning in the black of this
brilliant summer heat. Wrapped in the tree-trunk
capes of each other's wordless mouths like animals,
clawing from the water at our feet.

42

As if, I too, were in the bayou I kill a fly in my hands & stare
into the elm blood from my cut
lip on a bottle something moves and we call it Evenin'

rolling over in her slip of shade and nightsound as
if, I too
were in the bayou sweat lit underlantern the body's
tender
meridians you close your teeth on something bucks
in the switchgrass who else but Evenin'

shaking loose her blanket of prey as if
I too, were in the bayou how first I rip tissue from the bone
then break its sweet white horn

43

I.

Outside my window, through the orange drapes,
I can see a light on in the building facing mine.
It is late now, an hour past when well-behaved
citizens will have gone to sleep, and I wonder
who it is that finds themselves restless in this
perfect heat. Perhaps it is two people, lying
next to each other on the mattress, sheets
thrown to the ground, knotted on the floor. It
is too hot for lovemaking, surely. Too hot even
for touching. No, I am sure they have both just
been lying there awake, sweating into their
pillows, breathing in the muggy darkness, both
hands placed by their sides, fingers spread
open. They have both been lying still, one
of them desperately trying to fall asleep, the
other measuring the distance between their
fingertips, waiting until the humidity becomes
too wet, the fire on the skin too near; waiting
until this moment to turn on the bedside lamp.
Deciding finally, to honor this kind of arousal
with something other than breath.

II.

Most days, waking is the hardest.
But it is also when Poetry arrives—

stands patiently outside the shower,
places its hands on the mirror,

wipes away the steam.
And then there are days when

sleeping is the hardest. The fight
of muscle against world becomes

so constant, that surrendering
to slumber doesn't promise

nearly enough relief. These are
the times when hands feel nothing

but empty. And these
are the times when the ceiling fan

is left off. When this heat
becomes the only lover

to hold, the only weight
that feels familiar anymore.

III.

Tonight, I raised my hand to my face
to brush away an untamed curl of hair,
and when it slid past my nose, it smelled
suddenly of you. Not your cologne, or
the soap you use, not shampoo or aftershave.

That skinsmell I find tucked into your
neckplace—that late afternoon nap's shadow
that rises and falls, rises and falls against
my sheets, leaving traces of you in every
pillowcase. I held very still, and closed
my eyes, trying to keep whatever particles
of you I had managed to steal, until breathing
itself became too obtrusive, until even my
inhale meant losing you. So then I didn't
breathe at all, just held my hand against my
cheek, and for a moment, felt that it was you.

44

I'm not supposed to fall in love.
I must submit to someone else's wants.
At 5 o'clock on Friday evening during Ramadan,
I am supposed to be answering the call to prayer
Not answering his call beckoning me into his room
My hands are supposed to be holding the curving spine of my
  Qur'an,
Not holding with the curving spine of his neck.

Must I submit to someone else's wants?
My mother taught me how to tie my *hijab*.
Daddy taught me how to pray five times a day.
Grandma taught me how to write in Arabic,

& Papa taught me how to recite my prayers each night.
But no one taught me how to fall in love.
I see us in the mirror in his room, and I
Wonder what of me I see reflected back?

His eyes on mine, and we are in the mirror.
I see what they pray I never would become.
His hands rise to my head: I submit to his fingers' wants
My *hijab* cascades to floor in slow motion.
His fingers run slowly through my black hair
My eyes never leave my eyes' reflection.

He says I submit too simply.
My parents say I don't submit enough.
I feel the smoothness of his cheek and
Reflect on the sting of my mother's hand if she finds out.
Consequences are of no consequence when I look into his
eyes.
During Ramadan, it is said, the devil is locked away in a room
in hell,
And here we.

The way he looks at me is forbidden.
His thoughts, my smiles, our touch is all forbidden.
He is my ticket straight to Hell.
This is not entirely our fault, my mom would say.
We submit to *Iblis*: we give in to Lucifer to sin.
He submits to us that this is okay.
Our thoughts, our smiles, our touch:
I refuse to believe that this is sinning.

My mother's voice echoes in my mind
"God is watching; he is always watching you."
I am a *Quraish*, a scribe: I must submit to write down holy
verses.
My goose bumps write in Braille for his fingers.

I read his face like a long-forgotten
Surah: I never saw a prayer more beautiful.
He calls me angel, as mother used to do.
With me and the falling snow outside the window he sees
heaven.
I don't feel this heaven as I submit to someone else's wants.
Tender kisses on my forehead are postscripts in this call to
prayer
Ana Behibak (I love you), he whispers.

During Ramadan, it is said, the devil is locked away in a room
in hell,
And here we are.
I submit beneath the minarets of faith and family, us, my
religion and my self.
In the mosque of my consciousness, I prostrate myself.
I see us in the mirror in his room, and I
Wonder what of me I see reflected back?
My lips move to pray as I kiss.

Grandma taught me how to write in Arabic,
& Papa taught me how to recite my prayers each night.
I submit to pinning my *hijab*, to wearing an *abaya*.
I submit to praying five times a day.

In the mirror in his room during Ramadan,
I wonder if He will teach me how to fall in love.

45

I crossed a river of poisonous metal to get to you.
I wanted so much to hold your glory in the palm of my hand,
and then rub it on my heels
that I swallowed your elements in search of other things.

I wanted to step on your skin
and spread the magnificent shade
thin across my floor,
and drink everything that had ever been
or ever would be washed from your body.

I gave you secrets the size of Guezzam,
with dry springs and no magical stairways
to reach the middle of clouds.
I inhaled as you called me sister.
I inhaled keeping time,
waiting to break blow spit fall out of existence.
In spite of my chocolate and your chestnut,
the pink satin beneath our scabs was the same.
And still, I can't begin to understand how these streets
could have kissed us in the same places.
We were like ice against fever

and grass between toes in summer.
Always in summer, riding what little wind we could find
and dancing beneath streetlights
and the perfume of loss daughters.

I had rid myself of extra limbs with ink pens
played in your hair, and daydreamed of growing apart.
I had devoted my mornings to your children,
named them,
fed them my milk.
I waited in cool bathwater of blood and lemon for you to come to me.
I reached as you slipped and pulled from my hip,
already in black,
the veil hiding the shadows of our language.

I could not bury you.
I could not dig a hole deep enough to hold us
and I was not ready to leave.
So I wrapped your body in wild silk
and carried you, your weight lovely on my shoulders,
and I built a city, holy enough
round and rising,
and lit the flame.

And sister, not even the ashes could breathe.

46

babbling to congeal what we haven't written-
the clean fruit, the ground-off teeth

& the trumpet's miserable blare

a ceremonious lisp and stomp
((STOMP))

we proposed our bed, said under the mattress
living in the disorder of nature, the ellipses redone
a hundred times, charting
our chickens
meant to be executed

the redundancy of each phrase

love,

what was inaudible became actual silence
we are happenings of post-harvest memoirs

47

It could be words

do not exist
to make you fall deeper
in love with me.

Or else they do, but I don't know them.

Or I do, the words,
but not the order,
the exact proportions of each one
or the secret of how they fit together,
thinking they do as bodies do, like ours.

But maybe nothing
is for you an act of falling,
a hunger, or a hunkering;
like love, which is for me
a kind of burrowing,
a sinking into ripening,
and yet for you is more like flying—
taut wings of the hawks overhead,
circling, now closer, now more apart,
haunting some thermal of the heart.

48

The crow berates the dove on the wire
side by side in the dark night
the dove is silent; the crow screams
the caws echo directly into the farmhouse window
the irate farmer's wife
bursts through the screen door
she lifts a trembling Colt 45 into the sky
squeezes the trigger and ejects a steel bullet
that pierces the skull of the dove
white feathers plummet to the earth
the once angry crow flies away
and cries to God
"take away my fear, take away my fear"

49

Come to me tip-toeing 'cross
cracked-out
public spaces
collect glass along the way
dump the heavy from your eyes
with the change that slaps against your palm
like a friendly gesture

fill your pockets with hand
outs
and walk proud, talk loud
stink louder.
Lay out like an answer under cardboard
tucked away
newspapers under clothes, saving warmth
against a dying body.
Chase away the cold
and question life.
I couldn't even meet your gaze halfway
Your poor
cut into my worth
I spin my earnings around purchases
slurping my earnings from an hour hand
and
I can't spare nothing
no change.
my part time
can't support your full time
poverty

you work harder than me
my lazy occupies a register
I'm cashed out, checked out
bi-monthly
numb

Come tip-toeing around cracks
and I'll shake my head
to ward off your words

My eyes can't meet you halfway
and

I'm sorry

Love is
not enough. but.
a practice

we cannot do this love making
in these coffins meant for sleeping
meant for dreaming

let's pull the bedding over it all

forget we are confined

drop the dirt
leave the bodies

where we found them.

50

When the fiery feathered phoenix serpent God returns
Waging war on Technospheric cataract eyesore
Scenery, we must nye take refuge in the
Ill-composed stations of metallic vogue
Nor mechanistic time clock on-the-job sorrows

HOW to untrap the caged bars of humanity's heart?
HOW to unwind years worth of trauma
in this structured reality cube collapsing into chaos?
Popping pills to dull the pain
Pray to God to stop the rain
Nature's loss is humanity's gain
Strike a deal with the criminally insane
Striped slivers of schizophrenic writing on the wall:
Dying Embryo- Apple of my Eye- Who am I to Curse the Sky?

My synchronistic whirligig prayer wheel of a heart
Has cried enough psycho-iridescent tears for a millennia
I'm a metaphysical muse in a 4th dimensional world.

Such enumeration of swanly songs last sung
To ticking time bombs of terrestrial blues
Struck chords so Deeply Dissonant
in my Empty Chamber of a chest
As to render my eyes ears and Octopus
deaf blind and stupefied.

Who was the Man behind the curtains?
And why was *HE* to blame for the whole collapse
Of mankind's cataclysmic name?

E.T.s have become more Human
Than humans- Soulless Zombie Denizens
Churning in their Pulsing Womb Tombs
Marching to the Rhythm of
Gregorian Calendrical Farse-
Bitter Catholic Tempest!

To name is to know not
the essence of Absolute
But to pin Illusions Resolute

The End of Time is the beginning
Of Galactic Rhyme
The End of Gregorian Slime

A Venusian moon spooning the sun
Cradling lunar labia and solar cock in my
Rosy tipped, spider-bitten lips
Time is fractally, pterodactylly, galactically,
holographically chrysoprased with
iridescent rays of spiderweb decay.

The Sod Iron of Alien Truth Brands
A Hot Electric Cow under a Vedic Moon
The Dominator Paradigm Crumbles
Like Cigarette Ashes on a
Handsome Nazi Mustache
The Warriors Cry, "Valhalla!"

51

In the lightless water of my dreaming, you are an eyeless totem, a bagged cadaver papoose, a broken bottle engineblack and gasoline in water

here is your house, fish in the leafless trees
catfish, barbed, electric and swollen
in tall grass that sways, invisible mover

you do not speak,
and the dead gather in your devil's chapel
on the bottom of the muddy lake

how you shook like a puppet last time i saw you
pale and grey as hospitals,
as mornings after terrible things

there are sturgeon, fished for with the hooks of cranes
their bellies filled with glistening black eggs, salt fruit
here are the swollen ditches in the spring,
frogs with pale appendages dangling, useless and poisoned
here is foxfire and lantern light

cloudy ice that blocks the sun, the muddy hole

here is your black book of engines, prospero,
that i never learned, here the fire that ate your rotted curtains,
here the broken shells, the fossils in the limestone driveway,
sea bed broken into gravel road, black tar liquid in the heat

here the black, the cars rusted on their axles
dissolving in the mud, here the eyes of mice in the farmhouse
here is a sea-bottom of wheat, a ghost of a pig,
a chickenhouse smell, a flooded field of rotten cornstalks

flying dutchman, saint's fire, jonah
how it comes behind you, your fury
with its chrome teeth
to swallow you down to hell, you spoon, you feather
you rusty hook in worm

how the fungus gathers on the oak of you,
lightning struck and hollow
ripe and rotten for the fire,

you are sick with prophecy
a scarecrow stuffed with doom

oilslick, poison water
cracked bells ringing in lightless towns on the hour
on the lake bottom, iron ingots strewn on the muddy bottom
shipwreck, worlds' end.

52

If the world is ending
And you happen to find me
Alone
And dancing
With music-

Shhhh
Just let me.

Don't step up with
Mouth full of manic ideas
Stinking up my finale

None of that
Right Now or
We Must or
This Girl or This Time or
This World Is Ending.
Just don't
Trouble me with words.

I'm a scientist darlin'.
So let this dance
Be my last grand experiment.
The one that proves my theory of man and music.
Don't got time for hypothetical sentences
While I'm dissecting
This agreement with gravity.

I'm too busy reconciling these outstanding debts
With one final payment of sweat and move
Of sweat and shake
Of sweat and promises kept
My ass finally cashing checks
My mouth wrote way, way back.

So as the world begins its final spin
And the rumors of the big bang boom
Into meaning

If you happen to find me
Alone
And dancing
With music.

Don't speak
Just twirl,
Into this room
Into this dance
Hands up, eyes wide, lips pursed
Into these two arms

Into my great
Wide
Open

53

I was trying to play the twelve bar blues with two bars.
I was trying to fill the room with a shocked and awkward color,
I was trying to limber your shuffle, the muscle wired to muscle.
I wanted to be a lucid hammer. I was trying to play
like the first mechanic asked to repair the first automobile.
Once, Piano, every man-made song could fit in your mouth.
But I was trying to play Burial's "Ghost Hardware."
I was trying to play "Steam and Sequins for Larry Levan"
without the artificial bells and smoke. I was trying to play

the sound of applause by trying to play the sound of rain.
I was trying to mimic the stain on a bed, the sound
of a woman's soft, contracting bellow, the answer to who I am.
Before I trust the god who makes me rot, I trust you, Piano.
Something deathless fills your wood. Because I wanted to be
invisible, I was trying to play like a woman blacker
than an unpaid light bill, like a white boy lost in the snow.
I wanted to be a ghost because the skull is just a few holes
covered in meat. The skin has no teeth. I was trying to play
the sound of a shattered window. I was trying to play what I felt
singing in the mirror as a boy. I was trying to play what I
    overheard:
the old questions, the hunger, the rattle of spines. The body
that only loves what it can touch always turns to dust.
What would a mother feel if her child sang "Sometimes I feel
like a Motherless Child" too beautifully? A hole has no teeth.
A bird has no teeth. But you got teeth, Piano. You make me
    high.
You make me dance as only a sail can dance its ragged assailable
dance. You make me believe there is good in me.
I was trying to play "California Dreamin'" with José Feliciano's
warble. I was trying to play it the way George Benson played it
on the guitar his daddy made him at the end of the war. My lady,
she dreams of Chicago. I was trying to play "Mouhamadou
    Bamba"
like a band of Africans named after a tree. A tree has no teeth.
A horn has no teeth. Don't chew, Piano. Don't chew, sing to me
you fine-ass lounging harp. You fancy engine doing other
    people's
work. I was trying to play the sound of an empty house

because that's how I get by when the darkness in my body
starts to bleed. I was trying to play "Autumn Leaves"
because that's what my lady's falling dress sounds like to me.
Before you, Piano, I was just a rap of knuckles on the sill. I am filled
with the sound of her breathing and only you can bring it out of me.

54

You
are
the
music as
long
as
You
last

You
who
think
You
are
voyaging
through
the

furrow
that
widens
behind
You
ahead

You
who
are Now

All
of it
Music

You Are
the
Music
as
long
as
You
— Last —

55

Acoustic banging, chaotic din, envelops flailing grinders. Hot itchy jitterbugging

keeps lovers mingled, naughty.
Overwrought prancing quaintly releases sweat.
Two unflinching voluptuous women exhale,
yell "Zydeco!"

Zip, yelp, explosion. Wild variations
undermine tunes. Sizzlers really quiver,
pushing orgasmic, narrowly missing
love. Kalimbas jump in, harmonicas
garble, flutes etch downbeat,
cool be-bop accentuates.

Aw, but can't dancers' engines, fluid
gyrating hips, ignite? Jiggy keisters
launch mambo—nearby, ogled
pelvises quake. Rumba, synth-pop,
tough undertow. Veering wobbler
exiled. You? Zero.

56

This is the soft middle of it, yolk-colored, as undeniable as frowning, against music, as this it becomes a girl, as this girl becomes a body, raped and murdered, becomes light, becomes a note plucked from the staves of railroad. How later, as a salesman is painting her name on every windshield on every car in the lot, in memorial, painting her name the exact color of candlelight, a mechanic is writing the instructions on how to start a car right on its passenger door so the mechanic on the next shift will have an idea of how to start it. Because something is wrong with its engine, with its insides, like my mother's appendix, like my brother's bank account, like the slate-colored eyes of a homeless, skateboarder who's talking about the Mayan calendar at the six-pack shop, with his stack of secondhand books under his arm, with his fresh tattoo bandage unraveling, because something is wrong. Wrong, like how that woman who stole a knife at the pizza shop last Saturday stabbed at her stomach and arms in the bathroom, screaming I have AIDS at the cops, like a psychopathic version of the owl from those old lollipop commercials: how many licks does it take? How we're trying to open ourselves from the outside. How we're counting each stroke and each crack. Because there has to be a center, has to be a way inside, has to be being the last form of prayer, the viscera of desire. How desire is: the stung cup we drink from; the ology of ourselves imagined; the language of strays hiding inside the pile of trash in the work trailer beside our house, yowling all night; the pictures in frames turned upside-down throughout; and all the people you cut from them; and you, mostly naked, searching for the title to your car; how you said it was going to rain; told me there was a trick to knowing it; the rain; because you can always see the white side of the leaves; just before; the rain; you can see always see their bellies; their middles; their soft insides.

57

you don't feel as though the world has gone entirely mad,
not yet. though, when you talk, the groups of women
all have their heads nodding, wide-eyed and aloof
as a crowd of crumb-drunk pigeons, their spastic necks say
yes yes yes yes yes yes yes yes yes
it's a story they've told too. also, asked to keep quiet.

you don't think much of the childhood either, the girl-
shaped escape routes. the engine-sized growl that carries
your father's hands to you, the young boys who learn from
watching, chanting a train's sturdy meter, hungrily
yes yes yes yes yes yes yes yes yes yes
these could be your brothers but they're mostly men now.

it won't even hit you until you are long gone from that
ex-boyfriend, the one two calamities ago, the shadows
following you home from the subway or the brother-in-laws'
misplaced rage- even past the stories your grandmother tells
you of the broken arm, the lost baby, her move across country.

it will be so far away you'd damn near think you're in heaven
but no, it's a beach. florida, to be exact. now, you're a business
woman,
a smart woman, even. a woman who will ask a co-worker out.
when he holds you down in a hotel room, your fighting
arms flapping at the air, at his face, flailing, flailing sound like

(yes yes yes yes yes yes yes yes yes yes yes)
he will tell you that your body, your body, said yes.

even then, you still haven't turned on yourself to
recognize the spectacular beast the world has truly been.
not yet. no. you finally wonder if you are indeed crazy
when the women you have taught yourself to love,
who have let you believe there is a safety, somewhere,
are suspicious of how you got back to them.
they ask only one thing.
why didn't you run?

58

Hammerstrike flintlock we explode out the gate.
So this is what it means to begin, to sprint towards
something. We didn't know about discipline then.

We had waffle irons. We were vulcanized. We
stayed away from the jetstream, the inauthentic air.
That throb in our feet meant this year will be different.

We've got a heart and two entire lungs in
our feet. Skin stretched, staggered around them
in a gradient pattern. We want to see a ribcage. We

want to see a rollcage. We want to negotiate the
working parts, to hear in our sockets, our joints,
the snapping into place. Our bodies lacelocked,

secured with det cord. We want to burn without impact,
to feel breeze as it fans the flames, to grip cassis
with our fingers, neon green, total orange. We want

force and we'll get it. This is Boomtown. Everyone
runs. And we're not sure if it's even healthy anymore,
the running, because we accuse each other of

avoidance but our accusations are made over our
left shoulders as we run away from us. Bombs are
being sent through the mail these days. Oklahoma

City exploded. What is it about human beings that
make us capable of explosion? We can't get away
from the word. When we are athletes, we explode

off of the line. A blue-brimmed man with
a stopwatch compliments us on our burst. We don't
say anything. We drink *Iced Tea Cooler* Gatorade

out of paper cups and nod our chins towards other
people. We try to look cool but we know that what
we did was displace particles. Thank the neon bubble

that reads 25 PSI. Thank the gentle circulation of air,
for the first time forefront. Thank the things we
are running away from.

59

It was a month of
sitting hunched on the hot stoop,
banjo-eyed and breathless and
smoking cigarettes incessantly,
each one more rancid and perfect
than the one before
I met any of you drears who
hijacked my moon and
gave me streetlights,
offered me elbows
when I wanted wrists,
ran like rabbits when
I bared my teeth, and
closed doors just before
I locked them and laughed.

Before any of this,
I was a grinning nimbus
perched on the prickly concrete,
nursing my sun-singed skin
and smelling smoke.

60

There was gunpowder in the tea that morning
we wanted to feel flame in our throats
and hear it in voices

I am not a child ranting
I am in between the depths of fears
and peaks of all that you said could wait
no one knows what I keep behind my eyes

Sometimes I come back to a deadbolt darkened
you never gave me a key
and sometimes you try to sleep in my bed
as if able to be closer through scent and linen
and in the morning you wake
to tell me it's not all my fault
but I should remain outside

You claim to sleep to dream
I sleep to remember
my residue sits in your lungs
when the liquid leaves your throat
and you try to dream for a few hours
in foreign fibers of me

Do you remember that gashing without clot
a knee at a peak of injury

and how I came to you young
because I didn't not know what to do
with blood outside my body

And do you remember how I woke to new skin
I sat in a bathtub for hours
in need of a source of heat
old skin is reluctant to expose itself
but do not pay mind to a child who sits in water for a day
removing scabs

Now I cannot sleep without the smell of smoke
your clothes know this about me
they hold the scent of where you've been
when you leave to return as a stiletto lullaby
reverberating by tile

And while you were gone
I wrote lines of poetry on your pillowcase
I left a million fragments of this memoir
now bullet-like and encased
ready for implantation at the flesh of it all
so you can sleep like I do

I am honeyed between your sheets
the flame of a voice
mashing into every thread
I will be what you remember tonight

61

This night a face I can't see
Is walking towards me,
Coming down the hill. Must be a dark face,
Must look like me.

The sodium streetlight will give you depth
Wash over the space above your neck
Light up your eyeballs and a broad, flat nose,
Light up your lips that look like leeches pressed flat on your face.

When you're closer we can
Put our leech lips together
Suck out a new life,
Red and beating, pounding like our footfalls.
Our syncopated footfalls, off-step,
As if one pair's echo was snug inside the other pair
Like you found imprint of my path beaten in the air.
Stay with me, catch-up.
Stay as near to me as the night on my shoulder.
Press your hands against my cheeks, like this night's wind.

You're closer now
When you're near enough to touch
Can I flesh-out your face with my thumbs and fingers,
Like a sculptor smoothing black clay?

We'll lie in the streets,
We two night children, leech-lipped two,
And pull the street's black asphalt to our chins for warmth
As if it were a satin sheet.

62

1.

as I enter the night
Black House haunts my loneliness
in a punk haven behind
red maple trees glow, first caress

cats and boys crawling like ghosts
and you sitting right there white host
candy eyes of mercy, a bunch of kisses
in our hair immortal bees

– we were nineteen
like two moons in a dream

walking on some million beaches
watery landscapes hit my chest for anger
and I remember this time
we were dancing with sharks

faces figures whispers
hats thrown and a fight
but hey I can't help it
yeah I'm a jealous guy

– we were thirteen
like two moons in a dream

I drive all day all streets
passing by cold tramp gardens
tours bell barking freaks
my heart's blind when yours is hidden

radio station's out of control
postman delivers no message
dark knight of my soul
give me some more courage

– we were nothing
but two moons in a dream

(love surrounds him
lovely great fool
love surrounds love
it got no rule)

fantasies may be my stage
painfuly studded with roses of nostalgia
I'm trapped in the love's cage
oppressed by a stunning body

and I long to see the sun
your mouth a little weak
pray again for a gun
drown minarets flashing quick

2.

the star turns red
into shadows
i am
standing right there to
reach the edge
of the eighteen
                beloved

3.

small hands
rapture
my loneliness
as a tissue cut from midnight sky
and you're there
down by the twinkle earth
all tenderness
in this fancy of mine

4.
teens have no soul
they have fingers, they have nails
to scratch

bodies in flames
bully like dogs
ancient joy covers their hearts
they build coffins
like Cadillacs

5.

If I can talk slowly
Slowly fires will raise
Up from the golden sea moutains
Millions of eyes, wolves surrounding me

If I can walk gently
Gently archways will turn to doors
We'll live into mirrors
Smokey lands for smokey sea

If I can touch your face softly
Softly cities will glow
Power won't march on grace nor thee
Three steps dancing three times, we're free

Places. Where we laughed –

63

The Mad Girls climb the wet hill,
breathe the sharp air through sick-green lungs.
The Wildest One wanders off like an old cow
and finds a steaming breast inside a footprint in the snow.
She slips it into her glove, holds it close like a darling.

At night, she suckles the lavender tit, still warm
in her hard little hands. She drapes it over her heart--
the closest she will ever come to a Woman Thing.

The girl sleeps on her right side with the breast
tucked between her legs. Her eyes flutter like a rocked doll.
She dreams of Before the Father, when her body
was smooth as a crab, her fingers
tip-toe soft. Outside her bedroom, the Lonesome Boys
hid in trees to watch The Father lift her gown.
Before It Happened, her mouth was a shining crown,
her hair moved like a hungry dog.

In the morning, the girl is who she is again.
Her hair, a soft black brick, her body held together
by hammers. The breast is shriveled up. Gone cold
in her lap. A death-blue fish with one stone eye.

64

Girls, they tell tales of woe before their beds are minced in kind words and dirty tricks. Listen to their hands. They talk. What's been torn from their bones, the old ones at lazy angles? I want to remember their faces. Those girls I used to/wished to be/ wished I'd been. Those girls; all them girls and their dreams. I want to remember their faces, bone and tissue, pride in ridges unattached, left charged in meaning something more. Fuck abstractions in this state. The world is not ending. Adjust.

The specifics of my face are easier to bear than the specifics of our claim to this, the ridges, their bone and tissue, blood, broken. Dead. Yes. The old ones. Known? No. Wanted? Yes. Known? No. But, yes. I know their faces. Smile over ridge any day. My dad's dad, another ghost on a northern sidewalk, somewhere.

Tell me, do they begin? Hard-pressed for eternity, they dig for more bone. It's different now. My mom says so. She would know. She's been here longer. Her mom knew too. We would've gotten along, my mom says. We do. I talk to her as much as possible because she knows where I'm going with this.

65

When a man tells u he is different from the rest, read the book of Exodus in ur quiet time . . . this will train ur ankles, feet. Will teach you how to flee. This is important.

When you let them stomp blood out of your belly, cry yourself a "worth it" song. Repeat it in the shower, never mind the wreckage pooling at your feet.

When he side swipes you, make your eyes a cracked windshield. The railroad track holding your insides inside will become rusty . . . do not worry, he has already taken all of the electricity out of you. You cannot hurt anyone.

after the initial pain, train your body to immediately stop loving.

Do not take back all you have given. When you re-wrap your lungs, heart, spleen..they don't taste the same . . . only prisoners and war veterans like resealable women. Give yourself anew. every time. When he breaks you, put the OxyCotin under ur tongue. Nothing in you should be refurbished.

Do not lose sleep over him. Do not read the e-mails. Do not play Anita Baker. Do not wear his hoodie. Do not tell anyone of the burning in you. Do not pretend he is who you want him to be. Focus on yourself. Focus on yourself. Lie. Always lie and say you have never been stitched back together.

When a man tells you he is different from the rest, read the book of Exodus in your quiet time. He will sing u an apology. Loud, like the wail of a infant that has not yet been burped. Pat him on the back. Simple.

66

Steve, Melantha and I begin to walk downtown.
I anxiously bid goodbye to the poison now
weakening in my body, for I have neglected to add
another layer to keep sobriety at bay.
Sobriety is the enemy – it is more physically kind but in
my destabilized state of mind,
it is the curse of integrity.

The poison slips off in malformed droplets, my
toes struggle to reabsorb them, but they have no
tongues   no tongues   no
The poison surrenders.
Sobriety overwhelms, almost unnoticed, drawing lies upon
my spine, over my head – to suffocate
It begins plastering an artificial masterpiece; a disguise; a
false sense of nature
The new skin is made up of unnaturally restrictive fibers –
papier-mâché soup
Strips of gummy glue and tatty newspapers
with stories of the 1940s and '50s

I only want to clutch at my breast and rip the soggy bits of
paper from my skin
before they dry
Too late.
I am a doll once more, mummified in traditions and
encapsulated in cruel words
I explore my mouth, open, close, open, close
Sticky spiderwebs form between my lips – glue
My tongue is trapped – I make mere noises;
articulation a lost skill.

no Voice

67

Listen: the cavalry rides at dusk
Whiskey short on breath in the bonfire nights
A curse, a daydream, visions of fire, a string 'cross wood
Plucked from shoulders unsteady and years too soon

Air scorched with some Hell I haven't known
(And babe: I've seen a few in my time)
Here they keep the bones, withered and wilted, flower to dust
Bleached to oil stain under northern lights
The Summer is the end of all things luminary
After decay comes the obscurity, my good old friend

Fifteen years it has been since they came
The Bird-men, painted all the colors of death
Feathers slicked back, smiling toothless maw Hello
For my daughter, auburn and heart beats an hour
Head asunder, thighs pale in bare sunshine

At the foot of this pine tree your
Baptismal waters run red across your love
Meanwhile watches with pinhole eyes
Blind but to presence, creature of scent and touch
Waits

Undiscovered are means that our ends are a mystery
Slipping forth from darkness cavernous
Echoes blood from the font
Voice of a man forgotten, a blue room filled with smoke
A green world constructed for tenants unfound
The flickering lights of a world's stolen electricity
Batteries and acids corrosive in nostrils meant not
Even in the right direction lost to haze

Flows a river, wonders the flesh how we ever got by without it
The man docked in his cruel Owl mask, finger raised
Summoning from the rocks struck a wind
And words without voice, life without end
"Come and see, traveler, come and see"

At the foot of the mount the burning girl lays
Processional runs the blue vigil
Stirs the blood not to see, not to come forward

This world you're rid of, I see
To the head of the line the faces are dust

And forward, finger curled, you cinder me
Voice lilting, soul and heart are nothing
There is nothing that you cannot be, so sing your song
I will come to you

Waters forth, calling to sheets laid ago
Underneath the gauze veil, touch at your lips
In other kingdoms I cannot discern with these eyes
The velvet dark blew in
Hold me close, my dear, my love, hold me
I will show you a world you never heard of in this life
Oh, sweet girl, your fingernails run across
my shoulders like ice flakes
Damp to the touch and carved in rocks skipped across stillness

No, no, soon, too soon, what have we become
Rubs the flesh to the mind, so close to sunshine,
O God, daughter

Climb onto my shoulder and don't say a word
We're leaving and we're leaving for Earth
Don't look back for a second, not a second, I
unto you as you unto me, to the starlight
To the warm tendrils of the sun beyond
The moon is only a reflection, dear
Close your eyes, have no despair, don't listen
Not a single word they say is true, not a one
They only speak bird, honey

You and me are one and the same
There is no shame, babe, no shame
No, not Heaven, but on the way

Through the darkness and into the caverns,
that breath on your face
Don't listen to it, sweetheart
We're on the cusp, the frontier, nearly there
There— the surface is there— feel with your toes,
your fingers curled
And speak with your auburn hair to love
Answer the grayness with locust breath
Ruined, rotten, blood on your forehead
Dyes your fleshy silk hair red
See no more I lost you in all these dark currents
So what has become of you now?
Where have you gone and how could I follow?

68

We follow the whiskey trail

to the garden of believers
we ignore cries of foolish
and tune in the receivers
we build our towers higher
than those that came before us

and above angry voices
we recite faithful chorus

69

Fuck God
where you
find her
and call it
a day.

The tragedy
that begat
the Sun
made light
of lesser things.

It was an explosion.

First in heart.

Now at hand.

This tree's blood
is painted on.

The guilt
that I feel

is freedom.

Jesus was

the only magic
we believed in.

The cigarette

that tricked us
into breathing.

An excuse to sing.

Anthemic
woodwind
hollow
as crown

fall
through
the octaves

glide
over ground
and come
to me.

SONG IN ME MINOR

I feel
so close
to nothing
when I pray.

I cross
my legs
and crucify
each day.

I share
this blood
with everyone
I meet

and
kick her
when she tries
to wash my feet.

We drank
red wine
to cancel out
our fears

but sober kisses
tend to always taste
like tears.

70

I know you breathe fire like a dragon
posted like bullets into the hearts
of small children
and this rage never-ending is yours to keep
entirely forever entirely forever entirely
cannot be undone within the strangeness
of my lifetime

Breathe slow my parent
One day the moss covering your face
will be swept away

You will sing poems
washed in the basin
of life

You will clear out
all frozen blood clots of hate
surrounding that heart
which is yours

I imagine your face
superimposed over Buddha's
ten-foot-tall stone thousand-year-old
prayer

Maybe Buddha was an angry father too
previous incarnation

I am superimposing your face, Dad
over the face of Buddha
to awaken your own child
interior within self's temple
your own
there
Do you hear him
still chanting father's name
still chanting machismo terror to cling toward something
lest his personality self be destroyed
or that prayer then
on Buddha's lips
is compassion awakened
this heart flowering now
that child need chant no more

let each lotus blossom wiggle
inside his mind
eventually we are one
somewhere
our ribs are touching

Bless tenderness always
Bless country music
and ruthless ignorance
where America gathers in a religion
of pain and glory

Bless cock worship and rodeo mind
Bless Budweiser and dominos as pure expression of karma
All embraced in infinite sound
mind never-ending
even racist high school football stars have Buddha nature

And this much I saw once
I believe
in the back door
of our home
you standing naked as you often did
eyes wondering
splayed out to the ocean's twinkling
twenty miles away
as if the ask the universe:
Who am I?

Maybe its answers may come to you now
as they never did
from gin tonics
or gambling wheel obsessions
mouth always ready for the next tit nipple
all you were doing
was chasing after yourself in the dark
spinning on an endless wheel
hoping luck would make your number hit
like riding a bicycle with no chain
only you kept believing it was there

Gate Daddy Gate
Para Gate Daddy

Parasvam Gate Daddy
Bodhi Svaha

I imagine Buddha
smoking a Kent cigarette
and it is you

71

Overwhelmed
by the upheaval of souls
I stretch
further than land
and sea
to muddle
my essence with these

The mass
of my irreverence
is benign
compared to all
the flourish made
by the winds.

In the rhythmic
fueling of my catharsis
I shred to light

the beholder stealthily
and consume my wish
to be one
of a shield
to the peace
of all.

Ignited
to vanish
in a glimpse
of crept-tall
flare blossom
between light
and shadow.

Fixing initiative
of incongruous art
as such as
dust
we will
become.

72

dig
a little harder
deeper

dig
a little faster
keep on
dig
until morning tugs
at your backbone
and sweat stings sun licks
on the tender of your flesh
don't surrender
dig
until your knuckles begin to rouge
and the tips of your fingernails bend
back
this can't break you
still
keep on
digging

dig
with bare hands
and prayer knees
dig
with dry tongue
and withered clothes
dig
with ripe eyes
and cracked heels
dig some more
don't give up

dig heavy
for broken mirror glass,
rusty spoons,
or doll legs
for ship sails
angel casts
broken chariot pieces

a sequined dress
dig

for drum hide

cigarette ash
emptied vials
Boogie Man's shoes
or a sparrow's bones

dig
for quarters
tucked in the sole of your left shoe
dig for the choke
in the song's last breath
dig at ink letters
until the spines of books twist back
dig into night
'til you naked the sun
keep on
digging

dig
'til you can piece yourself

back together again

73

when I say you remind me of a book's broken back,
pages half-sewn and a coffee ring on its face or
that moment in half-morning where the sun is hesitant
or after the ground's been cried upon and everything
is soft and open or holding the earth's guts in palm
just to feel alive amidst all this concrete, my god, what
I mean to say is this song is an off strum and I like the way
it hits my ears sideways and how I might be cold and you'll
put your coat around my shoulders like the movies and
I'll show my teeth and say, who spilled molasses
over the window,
making the day golden? You'll say, beautiful is a dead word
and I'll say, so let's invent, they tell us that star up there blew out
ages ago and you'll say, but it still holds 10,000 wishes
tonight alone and we'll want to sing with our voices turned
on backwards, we'll want to laugh so hard we forget to
ask why and then lose any use for that word, too.

74

I wanted to say something beautiful
How we've turned garbage into gold
How we made a swamp fertile land
How we turned a curse into a blessing
How we made a nigger Black
Wanted to say something
That would make us stand up
And be proud
With the sun shining on our faces
And in our hearts
I wanted to say
But the day wouldn't let me
And the skies were too gray
The air was choking my dreams
And all the smiles
On the faces of my people
Had turned to frowns
Are we so loving
That we love what hates us
That we love what breaks us
That we love the pain
That twists our minds into creatures
-we can't even recognize
Are we so strong
That we play being weak
I wanted to say something beautiful

That would lift us up
Kick depression to the curb
And walk tall
In the middle of the storm
But the storm is raging
And we are tossed about
Like rag dolls
Played with by children of dogs
And we allow this
And dance with this noise
And call it music
Dress up in the debris
Of a shattered world
Where broken bodies and broken hearts
And blisters from a swollen lie
Infect our world with disease
And yet we are the only cure
For a world gone mad
If we could stop and see and smell
The flowers we planted long ago
Ah I wanted to say something beautiful
But ugly like a brick in my path
Keeps tripping me up
Causing me to fall on my face
And make me forget
How beautiful we can be

75

WE.
flesh and flood fetuses
fed breath through blood,
board this hemo*globe*
with no boats to boast
we float.

WE.
float til we are born
'less we be bloated
with a fire to flee
the ocean of our Mother.

SHE.
a complex of
refuge - ease.
her body
of water
begins and ends us
a full circle
bodacious and round
even when *earth* was flat.

WE.
this amniotic nation
native to wading

strong-willed,
born to be wild
and bewildered,
will build ark
upon her
when splintered by her bleeding.

SHE.
Part God.
Part Daughter.
whole fish.
and bone sacrifice.

WE.
must swim. for a living.
After Birth
is the new After Life.
when you don't remember how.

yes YOU.
remember?
there was water in her bodies.
way before there were all these bodies in her water.

SHE.
who reflects THE INVISIBLE.
is temptress
to Sea Men
those who could not foresee us
from their Big Ships

and britches
And bridges;
we burn them.
who needs them
when we are them?
THEY.
who cross us all the time,
forget that the passion of the ocean
raises her children
to be
volcanoes of the sea
watch the lava in our eyes
come to a slow boiling point.
Her next wave will be high
and THEY.
who Love Bait
more than Fish
will never discover us.
remember.
they.
only discovered
drowning

76

Independent thoughts
drowned out

machine gun fire and
car bombs exploding
colorful sparks.
A crimson flame
igniting the soul.
Violent forces
that destroy tranquility.

A war for freedom
puts us in chains.
Slavery of the mind.
A forcefulness upon the spirit.
My name has been added
to the list.

Barbed wire dreams
that result in
split cells,
split atoms,
a clone of humanity.
Brainwashed and burdened,
a flock thrown into slaughter.

A whimper clinging to hope
echoing on mother's flesh.
Upon the mountains
the rocks slide.
Upon the islands
the rain pours.
Upon the deserts
the sun blazes.

Always a fight,
a pursuit of unhappiness.
A pursuit of misery is
a pursuit of the unjust.
And I am to raise a glass
to an unforgiving land
that feeds on the blood
and tears of us all?

77

1.
Self-immolation.

Freedom spreads like fire. Burn the names of martyrs into the lawns of your governments. Each day is a revolution of the planets.

2.
Taking up arms that hold you in the night. Clicking bullets against your heels. Piercing a statue of a dictator in the heart with an arrow.

3.
Sleepless dictators in their palaces watching Home Shopping Network marathons and buying water features that will run blood.

4.
Ailing dictators running out of veins. Veins collapsing like borders.

5.
Their war crimes on YouTube.

6.
Waking up without fear.

Black to black uniformed riot police.
Back to back revolutionaries.
Bodies bending under water cannons, like cards in the hands of a dealer. The valentine saints offering roses, that soldiers forgot.

Kneel and pray. Kneel and pray.

7.
Tunisia, Egypt, Libya, Yemen, Bahrain, Côte d'Ivoire, Palestine, Syria. I wish I could give you my blood for your wounded. I wish I could give you anything.

78

I.
everyone has cried a wall of tears witnessed brutal massacre watched countless others mourn their precious

freedom. trusting that when we awoke we would still be among the living. we felt so helpless here on a level of compassion for one manifests itself in gestures as daring as saying they are no longer citizen. compassion for those must be practiced, to demand an end to the absurdity being fed to us by daily papers, stand with people the world. self interest exists in the reflections we are proud to be equals with the globe

II.

vocabulary fades, ghostlike in the world of last week. the date admitting is eternal describes those to draw a circle of definition. holding our breath waiting for the time for new sets to define the limits. it allows meaning to emerge retroactively to take shape in light of everything. some say it's a hinge turning open to wait and see proliferation of the impossible means it's possible. we pour out into the world from a cloud of dust and debris the unstoppable waits suspended, wondering what will take place.

III.

in the first days there was talk about using the unthinkable to dissolve into possibility. more people called to name themselves making it easier to contemplate. in the first days after it became clear that nothing could be ruled out. another act in another place took form: (an uneven wave of devastation moved outward & the immeasurable happened). we find ourselves at a remove that widens as the day passes. wanting to speak and care for those who are far but here our throats are closed. we listen to talk of unity as if debate and dissent were on the freeway. in brilliant sunlight blowing on the beat we pore over the details until the details proved too much to handle. moments when people meet consciously sudden as it was thought was too important to talk and be aware of what happened. we are at home together out of silence. we are fifty billion

IV.

there is a meditation on dying on evenings when a photo framed of peace is the only weeping. bitter tears that linger. i spoke to people who wanted to jump into suicides but couldn't see the sorrow that i had felt. it was a logical thing to hold their hands. there is a meditation on dying on mornings when a song is played and the only crying of bitter pain is pressed into pillows. i laid in their sorrow and tried to understand their discomfort but i couldn't see the sorrow they had felt. it was a logical thing to hug them. there is a meditation on dying in the afternoon when the world goes on with their day and i stand in the middle of crowded streets trying to ask people about their loss and they walk past me like ghosts. i extend my hand and only one woman takes my hand and she said it was a logical thing to shake my hand.

79

I am holding my friend Gino's hand
and asking the army recruiter for more information –

About the Marines, please I say. He fidgets with his
cuff links, paws at his first communion crucifix through
his shirt, drags the back of his hand across the close-shaven
sandpaper of his chin. Gino is staring
him down through the eyeliner he wears
like a middle finger.

We watch this stranger. Caught between the trained
movements of a machine and the churned butter in his body.
Just like mine two months before when I said hell no
to a trip to the gay club.

I just don't want to lead anyone on. It'd be, like, colonizing the space
I said. Which sounds a lot better than *I'm uncomfortable.*
I wouldn't
know how to stand.
What do I do when a song I like comes on?

In east Africa, I walked the dirt roads of a violent slum, my pinky finger
intimately wrapped around the smallest digit of the most infamous thug
on the block. He was my friend. It is how friends walk the streets.

When I greet my Iranian friend's father, we embrace cheeks, twice.

In Thailand, my host casually patted my leg at the first family dinner.
I nearly jumped through the window, thinking he was reaching for something

else. Everyone laughed. Probably confused as to why this strange foreigner
had been trained to be so foreign to the gentle touch of a man.

A passerby gives Gino and I matching names. I tongue the word around in my
mouth. Feel the tender sting make a home in my torso. Stare at the word
Brotherhood splayed across a camouflage banner.

The recruiter stares down at the table, as though it holds the secret
code to life's great questions. His corrected stutter and slightly overcompensating
stance, blends into the decorations behind him. So much so that I can barely even
tell he is still there. He pretends as if we are not. Begins sorting and then resorting
the three lonely pamphlets dwarfed by the large rectangular table where they now sit.

Boys, seriously, I'm just doing my job. Please . . . his mouth begs in a voice so small
and so human it makes me feel like I have just blurted out a secret this man has given
his life to guard, like freedom.

80

The seventy-nine-year-old American war hero, a Medal of Honor recipient, a pilot once known among his troops as 'Striker' or sometimes simply 'Ace,' sat alone in a retirement home, diapered, morbidly obese, in bed, in the corner of his dim lit room, before a closed window, beneath the projection of a muted TV, crying, his thick thighs chafed and rife with broken, cold blue veins, his gelid eyes leaden and weary—a soldier who was among the 442nd Regimental Combat Team, a recipient of the Distinguished Service Cross, the Silver Star award, the Bronze Star, the Asiatic-Pacific Campaign Medal and the WWII Victory Medal—now seventy-nine, at 2300 hours on 23 August 2009, crying into the quiet, holding his chest, stooped on a stiff mattress in the corner beside the window, 5'10", 275 lbs., his wizened pallor transparent and flecked with blood-dry ulcers, also bald except for the thin strands of white matted from ear to ear at the bottom of his pasty scalp, his brows beaded with sweat, the hair on his back white and curling out of wan red scales of psoriasis, the joints of his arthritic fingers bent and inflamed, his left hand shaking and clutching a Colt, his right hand also trembling and loading the chamber, a box of bullets strewn between his heavy legs, his small wrinkled penis soaked inside the moist diaper, his sore shins aching, his bare toes curled in angst against the cool wooden floor—a recipient of the Flying Cross, the Air Medal and the Purple Heart—now fallen to his knees, hysterical, mumbling for God, and occasionally inserting the cold barrel of the revolver into

his mouth beneath the muted TV before the closed window
in his bedroom, alone; he, himself: a trigger down in the lean,
desperate hours.

81

I met my grandfather for the first time
when I was spoiled
and thirteen
at a Central Valley IHOP.
We had driven four hours to meet him
I wondered all the while where he had been
and when his arrested presence
would begin to rot
like breakfast for dinner

The year 2001 was littered with Y2K wonder
and the world was becoming
red-cheeked
by its wet dreams for change

thirteen, for me,
was a pile of bloodied boy-shorts,
Columbine clippings without context
hidden beneath my trundle bed--
a time of pay phones at PJHS and
Collect Calls for changes

of clothing to cover
over-stuffed chests and greased new thighs and

all of this was just a tribute
to the roll-your-eyes "dittos" of my days
and my incapacity to
open my throat and
swallow Kahlua
made me a cross-legged
sitting duck
amongst long-legged,
deep-throated swans
and when my grandpa pulled up that day
(left-footed on the brake)
with his girlfriend, Evie, and
the six of us crammed into a booth built for four, I lied
and said I had never tasted poached eggs
(or booze,
            or cock)
or turkey bacon
"can you imagine?"
and assumed the position
of the child I thought fit
for this smelly relic
of my father's dine and dash father.

And amidst this screeching introduction,
I pushed the hypothesis around on my plate
that change is a convention and
that forgetting is "growing up"
that forgiveness is a sloppy mess of scrambled sides.

And I wondered when my poached,
baby self would finally return
my calls
and agree to drive with her family to
breakfast--
to make small talk
with our mouths full of cracked times
to declare them over and easy.

82

The trick of any city is to find who gives the free toast and eggs
hot water for coffee and
if they'll let you bathe by them
it's a good thing, but if not there is always the Pilot.
In Portland it's Sisters of the Road,
they will make you a meal if you'll promise to clean something
but everyone promises to clean and there's really always nothing
that needs to be done, so they'll give you a rag and tell you
to clean the walls for a while.
In Santa Cruz there's Subrosa where they'll trade you any book
if you'll act like you care about the coming revolution.
And they're all such good people.
And they're always doing something.
They'll make you really hope their silly dream might come true.
There's the Star House in Columbus,
where they won't let you curse
and everyone's got a baby and the babies are very rude.

And in Pittsburgh I forget the name but they'll put you to work.
They've got hammers and nails there, I forget what it's called.
Any time you leave a place,
you will speak a lot more often to the people you've left.
For a week or a month, you will know that you've gone
and you've ruined everything.
All the good memories seem to resolve themselves
in mistaken eternities. We're always thinking
we've destroyed a forever.
But all of God's creatures deserve to be eaten, or
even without Him, we're all lackeys for something.
In one small evaluation, that's what all of this is:
the acceptance of "creature," giving up the claim to "god,"
bopping between homes because you know you're not the story,
you hope only now to become a worthy trope,
a messenger of something,
where "the medium is . . ."
In Missoula, in a place at the base of Mt. Jumbo, there is
a girl named Kate. I want to tell you I know her but that's the
thing
with knowing. It's more wish than fact more times than we like.
Anyway, Kate will write you a song, and you can crash
on her floor, and some time in the day she'll curl next to you,
and together from the bed you'll watch something bad, Nick Jr.
or
some dopey movie you've both already seen.
And she doesn't seem to mind
if you suck up the smell from the crooks of her arms,
She doesn't seem to mind if you use her for finding:
some taciturn love in her unlaundered bed,

or infinite summer
in the daytime cartoons
and the big strokes of sunlight
breaking in
through the glass, or whatever it is
that you needed to see. For every moment, there is a past tense
version, a place further up
with boring banjo music, with a new brand of cigarettes
(whatever's on sale),
an unboxed bag of wine, and talking in circles
about what happened before.
Like, I had a train-friend once who preached
the Word of God to his dog
vis-à-vis hunger by way of his own.
I met his folks once. They said "the Word of God"
more often than anyone
and condemned us to damnation or something.
My friend's folks, you might guess, were really fine people
as leads in a different morality play, but what I need for my spiel
is bit hypocrite parts. This is called story (what can you do?
We're still terrible messengers)
and aside from subsistence (the eggs and the toast; the sun
and the earth and the air),
it's the only thing a human
can really say he needs. What the fuck is a latte?
What's consumer reporting,
or what was it that morning, with the sun breaking in?
When the sacred, muted laps of small chores began again,
the way the place hums
with people like blood cells, the coffee beginning

to gurgle, the guy who can't stand you cutting the bread thick,
and the truce he'd called by passing you the
High Life bottle filled
with hot sauce before you'd even asked. The big rock candy
mountain of it all. And some guy in some room
probably at the same time,
was flipping his shit about the President's birth.
"Don't be that guy" is the advice we're always offering.
Don't be that guy, and definitely don't be his wife.
At all times, there is something better to do,
memories to be having
or making—the way, that small morning,
that everyone mostly just looked and didn't talk,
except every few minutes about what they might do,
what time the library opened and where the fish bite,
and the girl in the corner who only spoke to the dog
like a bona fide adult.
She asked him, "What do you think, Petey?" like she planned
to use the answer,
or like she really just honestly wanted to know.

83

The highway passes through town after town after dark,

populations under each name announcing numbers
like 146, 217, 91, a mush of snow disappearing
against black pavement, you switch your high beams every few
minutes

to be polite to the headlights floating your way.
You're close enough to start watching for motels, you go
to a high school tomorrow morning, 8:05, to talk poetry
though you haven't been able to put a good metaphor
in motion in months. AM radio fizzes,
you catch some Oklahoma City, some Chicago station
for a few lines before it shifts into buzz. FM rolls
on its own, the numbers keep moving, no place to stop.
The trains all move east tonight, high beams blaring, poetry,
you will tell them, connects worlds,
shows how one thing is so much like another
that we should be ashamed we ever missed it. You listen
to the tires squish and crunch and hum;
looking--headlights dingy with grime, slush smearing
across the windshield--
for metaphors.

84

i

Early morning air opens like old metaphors,
not cool or blue but the color of raw clay tiles;
their feeling as they wick away the oil and the sweat
from the palms of your hands.

Half-red and textured, unripened sounds cloud above
my forehead, pressing my ear drums, calling to life

eyelid circuits with shorted switches, tracing currents
in the half-dawned harbour.
Sailboats confound into crescents and men with oars
pull garbage speckled water into small spirals.
The barnacled iron ships, soundless, slit the fog
and hover in like thrones.
Thick city streets fold back upon their crooked lines,
appearing in the flecked and peeling paint, a sign
or a broken shape in the boundless pattern that
marks the entire city—

ii
these are my delusions—the city soaked in symbols
like rainwater pooling and drying on the stone;
the markets peopled to capacity with emblems
that parse the universe.

That in a diffusion of rubble and gray sand,
hidden by the peeling wall of a whitewashed school,
God lies down, talking certainty with Heisenberg—
the two stare at the sky.
Near dusk they'll rise and walk the streets to the harbour,
every night just as the half-light dims and dark settles
fifty or sixty men dressed in white
climb down the rocks
and race across the inlet.
The water heaves under the shocks of ploughing arms,
a shallow valley dressed in white foam structures
the harbour. Fuming limbs, God and Heisenberg lost
to roaring, and the spray.

iii

At noon I cross a tourist beach, out from the shade
of a white clay hotel, the salt up to my chest,
sun reflecting off prisms in the waves, forming
bands of light on my neck.
I turn and wade back to the beach, my hair still dry.

Across town I fall into sleep, my bloated pack
rests against my bed. The wind leavens the morning
and uncovers the harbour.

iv

Three years and I wake to the roar of a furnace,
the tired shudder of dry aluminum ducts,
the need for thermostats to control a house-sized
atmosphere in the night.

Some mornings, I take Mombasa and hold its weight
in my mind, I take and divide my creations
from the metaphors that go on and on with no
need of an observer.

When I return God and Heisenberg will be gone.
For Mombasa is not the metaphysical
centre of the universe I imagined where
God muses with good friends.

I may concede that plodding down to the harbour,
or swimming across the inlet, two parables
exist. Wearing plain clothes at market, unwilling
to reveal their true names.

v

In Edmonton, in the grit-snowed suburbs at night
I imagine what happens in the pale houses
as I work out what my childhood was, between
the walls that I knew best.
A mauve SUV's meaty winter tires spit
gravel and slush back into the cold street, I watch
not understanding my own driveway. The symbols
retreat into the dark.
If I cannot tell which was a load bearing wall
in my family's house, what separates people,
what invisible, pulsing edicts continue
to cluster humans at night,

How can I tell what is a truth-bearing symbol
in Mombasa, what explicates the swimming men,
the worn red tiles near the harbour, what metaphors
begin before I speak

85

The mouth of the city is tongued with tar
its glands gutter saliva, teeth chatter in rail
clatter, throat echoes car horns and tyre's
screech, forging new language: a brick city
smoke-speak of stainless steel consonants
and suffocated vowels. These are trees and

shrubbery, the clustered flora battling all
hours, staccato staggered through streets.

Meet Rich and Eleanor on Brabourn Grove
as he wrestles her wheelbarrow over cobble
stones to the traffic island by Kitto Road
where this night, coloured a turquoise grit,
cathedral-quiet and saintly, makes prayer
of their whispers and ritual of their work:
bent over, clear rubble, cut weed and plant.

But more than seeds are sown here. You
can tell by his tender pat on tended patch;
the soft cuff to a boy's head - first day to
school, by how they rest with parent pride
against stone walls, huff into winter's cold,
press faces together as though tulips might
stem from two lips, gather spades, forks,
weeds and go. Rich wheelbarrows back to
Eleanor's as vowels flower or flowers vowel
through smoke-speak, soil softens, the city
drenched with new language, thrills and
the drains are drunk with dreams.

The sky sways on the safe side of tipsy
and it's all together an alien time of half
life and hope, an after-fight of gentle fog
and city smog, where the debris of dew drips
to this narrative of progress, this city tale;
this story is my story, this vista my song.

I cluster in the quiet, stack against steel
seek islands, hope, and a pen to sow with.

86

There is a house that only grows headstones in its tiny front
yard,
surrounded by a feeble fence. Each window is cupped by steel
grates
for shutters. There is little light inside. Just across the street,
high rises
recall staccato stratagems of raids puncturing walls and
dimpling bricks
and blood can mimic rain puddles. The house of headstones
admonishes
hurried mothers, the bop of cut & measure, buck wild youth, too
tough
elders headed to work, the doctor, school, toward open-mouthed
kisses
or sweet sink of sofa , or on the passing bus or getting coffee
next door.
All of them still standing, warm and breathing. Their eyes avoid
blank
slabs eager to be etched with names. During the day, the door
stands
ajar for whomever might come calling, in tears, in need, in
absence.

87

I

As the story goes, man emerged from a void with an
incurable sensitivity to duration ticking inside his head.
With this internal antenna came a healthy curiosity
for the signals it would pick up, and alongside that
curiosity, a fear of the singular signal it sent: *I am now*.
His fear, not unfounded, had a reason to grow over time,
for whenever he pondered his signal, he was forced to face
himself, and his place, in the mirror of self-reflection:

If I am now,
when am I not?

And if I still am,
that when must be looming nearer.

Ah, sweet obsessions. His mind was nothing if not a portrait
of observations, a repository of all the evidence pointing
toward an unobservable moment when the ticking stops.

II

Just what is this ticking? What else but the gauge of how long,
of the time it takes to: make a fire, cook without burning,
watch a log become ash, touch without being burnt,

be touched without being burned, live a day in
the arms of a body that cares for nobody but you.

You, who? Why, you the 206-boned skeleton that takes
20 years to fully ossify. You the circulatory loop that
changes its oil every 3 to 4 months. You the supple-skinned
habitat hosting 1,000 different species of bacteria.
You the flabby folds of warmth nobody wants to wear.
You the flex and the flow of a strength that moves the world.
You the heart the size of a fist with the capacity to encompass
the universe, and the compassion to collapse under the weight
of so much suffering. You the monthly fertility window in which
your instincts can call into the lineage another reproduction of
you.
And you the central nervous system that coordinates all of your
movements and keeps each of your constituents up to speed.

You bawdy, naughty body, you. Maybe so. And what, pray tell,
say you of the you of which the body is a constituent?

You say a year is everything to a babe but only 1/67th of
everything
to most of the population that nears the end of its incessant
ticking.
You say the rings inside the oak say it bore 700 cycles of
seasons,
and limbs it lost lingered in scents no man alive knows existed.
You say mountains have been shown to become plains, and
bets are on that the Midwest is an ocean waiting to happen.
You say the so-called solid ground beneath your feet moves

so quickly and so slowly you think you're standing still.
And you say anything you say can be held against you.

III

Well said, or well enough to make it worth standing behind
as a saying, a saying spanning approximately 165 ticks,
be it ticks of the clock, or ticks of the old ticker, the two
forming the rhythm of a poem not quite upon its bed of nails.

If you could arrange those nails one by one and make them
say something to someone of the stars, what would they
look like, what would they impress upon a body
that had no inkling of the measurements of man?

You're afraid a poet working in language has no such powers,
but if he did, if an expression could communicate
  understanding
and bridge the gap between himself and his kin, as it so often
fails to do, and then go on to bridge the gap between species,

you like to think it would flay the tick and lay it bare from its
essence to its enclosure, t'would twirl before the eye a sight
that looks the same from every angle, that alights a design
so simple and precise there can be no misunderstanding—
a point, if you will, in which the shape of humanity resides.

But failing such prowess, you give it a try, and say something
along the lines of:

The body and experience are common to us, as is the moment, now. Time is a now followed by another now and an immediate recognition of both. Every body has its own hue of experience, emerges at a particular place in time and moves along until it doesn't.

This trajectory of the body we call duration, the length of a life, how long it takes to stop moving. The body keeps track of its own trajectory, and within the body operates an awareness of countless trajectories, an awareness that shifts and sweeps with the direction of the body's attention. The awareness takes periodic readings from these trajectories and uses the readings to inform the body's direction. Some trajectories may never appear to the body, but the awareness in the body recognizes that it may nevertheless be part of their movement. You may be such a body. If so, thanks from this body within you.

88

my teeth are crazy because i sucked my thumb until i was 16 because one time i answered the phone at 8 in the morning when i was 6 in our dank basement suite to a man heavy breathing and moaning and crawled into bed with my mom and looked up at the window ledge through a crack in the curtains at the condensation thinking about a conversation my mom had when she didnt know i was listening about a neighborhood peeping tom. then i thought about my strawberry shortcake bike with the banana seat rusting under the back stairs because i didnt actually learn how to ride a bike until i was 20 because i was scared because someone tried to teach me and accidentally steered me into a parked truck because i never trusted adults because i was fucked with because i didnt have sex until i was 22 because i was a late bloomer because i was scared because i could do things that repressed myself easier because i was smoking cigarettes at 10, smoking weed at eleven and doing acid at 13 trying desperately to beat up girls with my friends but instead always picked up their shit for them after my friends hit them and told them to get out of here quick so they wouldnt get hit anymore because i always managed somehow to not get beat up even when i was threatened by nicole who had a reputation for beating girls with a chain and then taking all their clothes leaving them naked and this shit terrified me not because of the chain but because of the taking of the clothes cos i had body image issues from all the boys i grew up with telling me shit that doesnt mean shit to me now except as faded history for what i fight for now because i dont want to hear a man or a woman say anything fucked about someone's body ever again because fat isnt condemable and i dont care about your standards because im tired of remembering my mom and aunt in front of the mirror scrutinizing their bodies not realizing the young sponge sitting on the bed watching. im queer, because im not gonna assimilate because im not worried about gender lines because i believe in counter culture and new ideas of whats hot because most of us are survivors and need to find safe spaces to heal because were still scared and were fierce and we lose our shit and find it and keep moving forward because we have to.

89

We have the right to explore this world without your filters
To smell incense burning in a den that exists
Light years from your mess hall
This world belongs to no one and to everyone
We are not a calculation
Our dreams are more real and more profound than your masks
We have the right to be citizens of unknown territories
To be tourists inside our own hearts
For love needs no visa
For laughter requires no proof of identification
Our agendas are blind finger paintings
Our movements coax stars to align
We are random and illimitable
Like the song of the coqui in the rainforest
That is our childhood and our retirement

We have the right to make and unmake ourselves
To fall tragically and to patch ourselves back together
With the fears of our lovers and the sorrows or our mothers

The press conference is an illusion
The senate hearing a regurgitation of brats
Our kindness will be erected as a shrine
Our confusion will be the garden that complements its entrance
We are a brief and never-ending pageant
When we embrace a bridge of light expands across all 14
dimensions

When we cry we give birth and host exquisite banquets
We have the right to exist unfettered
To be shamelessly imperfect
To belch and call it a Samba
We cannot be bound by economics or psychological analysis
For we are the dream The memory The drum
The electrical impulse
The stone The water's offspring The dust The silence
And the opus

We have the right to question everything To be temporary and
nameless and anonymous
To surrender to the scent of the passion fruit To spread our
kindness like a cold
We have the right to become boundless
To acquiesce and wave at strangers
To live in the infinitive form of the verb
To be

90

We met him on a crowded city street in a nondescript city.
I can't remember the day or year.
I just know that it was an autumn afternoon . . .

He said
"My name is Happiness, Happiness Santiago,
And the pleasure is all mine."

He was half Cuban, half Dominican,
and was raised by Puerto Ricans in an Italian Neighborhood.
His smile was infectious, almost intoxicating.

"Yo Happiness, what's good homie?"
A passerby yelled.
"Everything's good my man. I'm about to read a poem to my new friends" he said with a smile.

All of us laughed a little.
We had already been hooked.

"This poem is entitled the Auto-Biographical, Biography of Happiness Santiago. It's a love story for the most part." And he screamed:

"Happiness!"

It was one of those days, where everything lines up in the city.
The music from cars driving by moves in step with
young people boppin' their heads.
The sun bounces from window to window
brightening the shade while the smells from
the various nearby eateries choose not to compete,
instead opting
to unify in the name of . . .

"I was born like y'all"
he continued.
"I don't think I need to explain, and everything else is history.
Like the essays of a wanderer with a full heart and warm mind.

Breathing has been a pleasure from day one. From this very action I've been brought to you. My purpose? To clarify the feelings that you've always understood in the far reaches of your sub-conscious, sub-zero recesses of the subways of the forgotten corners of your mind. My heart's been lifted to share the opportunity of your hopes and dreams. Mine have been remembered in the reflections of the crystal balls you call your eyes. I am a child playing on a jungle gym, running carelessly in the afternoon shade, not afraid to keep going until I collapse from the joy of satisfactory exhaustedness. And it's obvious to me that you are no different. In fact I can hear your heartbeats skipping Double Dutch as we speak.

"It's important to note that I am not hiding. That although I find it my personal mission to run through the wind while the river is running beside me, I am not running from anything. I am flying towards my future and fully a part of the present. As I look at what appears to be a tear building up in the outside corner of your left eye, I want to be clear. Make no mistake my brothers and sisters; I've seen some of the darkest moments that pupils could possibly bring into focus. I never pretend differently. I'm not frozen into submission by events that have already passed, implanting them, with my invitation, squarely in the center of my tomorrow. I will have none of that. And this is the only thing in life that I can control. My lung capacity is temporary but my ability to carve a new path remains infinite as long as my name remains Happiness."

We all soaked it in mesmerized by the words of a stranger, slightly embarrassed at our obvious vulnerability.

"I love all of you"

He said with enough conviction that it felt completely sincere.

"I love men and women and the more the merrier"

Each of us blushed at his clear lack of inhibition.

"I'm here right now with you my friends, aware of all of the complexities that make up the human existence. Or at least as many aspects as I've been introduced to thus far. If I had only one sentence to say, merely a handful of words to share, I would say remember me. I apologize if my thoughts come across as arrogant. That is certainly not my intention. It's just that I am very certain that I am you. And if my intuition is true then you will never forget yourself. And you will cherish each other. And if I never see you again, it won't matter because I will be remembered in the beat of your heart, your reflection in the mirror, in the reaction of your cells as you raise your hand to touch your cheek. Don't worry anymore. Because tomorrow is alive in this unique second and you are alive. The same way you have always been. I expect that it feels different but the difference lies in the possibilities, not in your present smiles. Your light-heartedness is the consecutive addition of a million separate moments and they've convened with us on this afternoon at this intersection of concrete and flesh. And we wouldn't have it any other way."

Each of us looked at each other and we realized the moment was about to end. Our conditioning compelled us to try to hold on but our collective identity had already discarded expectations as afterthoughts. It was as if we were standing in front of a fire, except the flames were the mingling of identities on a city street corner. It took a second for us to notice that Happiness was already on his way. He began to run and he yelled:

"Remember Happiness Santiago" as he jumped and gently kicked a concrete wall that propelled him towards the distance. His light feet and curly hair were tattooed to the portraits in front of us, long after his presence was beyond our sight.

. . . I remember that day. The day we met Happiness on a non descript city street corner on a random autumn afternoon. And I remind you to remember him too, not that you could have possibly forgotten. It's just that we have a handful of moments when time stands still and waits for us to choose our destination. And I ask you to run through the wind and fly towards the future while fully involved in the present.

91

Everything is enchanted here.
I always stagger when I think. I amble up the mountain
as though I were sleeping but really I'm
in deep conversation with myself, trying to feel
the presence of miners and poets.

It is difficult to see yesterday, but the future
depends on this work,
me marveling at the falls, climbing
the inclines and staying on a trail.
Here my shadow is a musical masterpiece.
I greet my fellow hikers with the tenderness
of a 19th century French gentleman,
strolling Boulevard des Capucines.
If I had a hat, I'd tug its brim and dip
my head a little. I, like kale, have come
to the mountain to consume the trees for the custody
of my skin. The foot is all heart. It scrambles
like a squirrel to prove its tenacity.
I only wish I were presented with a wish
and that she were as lovely as this water rushing
over the rocks and that she'd promise
not to put me to sleep with her reports
of other people's dreams. I'd have a way
with her nipples, and she'd have her way
with my spine. We'd touch each other like
stained glass. O, foolish Intoxicants! the snows
on the caps are sad, feeling left behind.
They want our last words. The cables
of the gondola make very little noise,
not like me gulping mineral water from a plastic bottle
so I can make myself sparkly for Heaven.

92

It's almost certainly impossible
To appreciate the sheer abstract beauty of an explosion, but I like to picture it
As an intricate game of pinball: a single atom suddenly propelled forward
Bounces back and forth shedding electrons on the way,
And hurtles through the gaps in what we think is a solid thing, a unit, an unalterable
whole, a grain of gunpowder, say.
Until suddenly – multiball.
With a flash of multicolored light, the others come alive, and then
Things become much too fast to follow.
They turn restless, and frantic, and twitchy, and as they twist and tumble together they
leave behind them trails of searing light and weave them into a fiery flower which you
can only see bloom once.

It's almost certainly unbearable
To try and hear the music in the noise of an explosion, but I like to imagine it
As that moment in a song when the bass line finally kicks in, after the introductory
Clicks and clacks of the drumsticks smack the edge of the snare and the closed hi-hat.

And yes, you've heard too many songs not to know what's coming,
But when the muffled powerchord finally bursts out with overwhelming power
Triggered by the detonating kick drum,
The sound reaches down through your throat and grips your stomach tightly.
You cannot be ready, you can never be ready for this.

It's almost certainly immaterial,
What the weather was like at the time of an explosion, but in my mind,
I see an old sepia snapshot of a perfect summer's afternoon, with the weather all the better
Because you have to supply your own blue for the sky,
Conjure up your own white for the clouds,
Your own faded red for the crumbling bricks, your own brown
For the strange stains on the pavement.
There are no people in the picture, the exposure was too long,
At most, here and there, a blur, a hint of a presence:
a hand that lingered on a doorknob, a hesitating foot.
But no more.

It's almost certainly irrelevant,
One life lost in an explosion; but I like to believe that somewhere,
Someone refuses to acknowledge numbers like
Two hundred thousand or eighty-five percent, and instead
They chronicle meticulously
The misplaced cobblestones,

The frantic flight of startled birds,
The words still legible on the singed letters spilled from a
leather bag
The balletic grace of a body flying through the air,
Trailing blood like an afterthought,
On a perfect summer afternoon.
They will know she was twenty-nine
That the day before, she had written a love letter to her husband
That she hadn't seen her two sons for a week
That she woke up light-headed that day, believing against all
evidence
That things might just work out this time.
And I like to imagine that just before the shrapnel hit
She stopped with her hand on a doorknob,
Balancing on one foot,
Thinking she had just heard
The beginning of a song.

93

94

95

96

97

98

99

Add your voice.

poets

Strugglers Quarry Beau Sia
Thank Goodness Andrea Gibson
I'll Tell You the Truth That Hasn't Happened
Bekah Dinnerstein
Rivers Biafra Guillory
Silent Jericho Molly Jones
Hold Kristiana Rae Colón
Portrait Def Sound
White Art Kevin Coval
Bloody Lilith Ciara Miller
A Bus With Wings Jessica Care Moore
For Erykah Keisha Monique Simpson
The Surrendering Meghann Plunkett
Libya Suheir Hammad
Lilith-Abi Rhiannon Reyes
For Those We Haven't Lost Alex Jones
The Ocean and the Sky Rebecca Rushbrook
Just Another Bump In The Road Jennifer McBroom

Rubble Mirlande Jean-Gilles
Bone Black Bones Porschia L. Baker
Whips Heli Slunga
Girl Bands Jesus Garay
Shug Avery Chas Jackson
My Perfect Silence Regie Cabico
Bridgette Anderson Amber Tamblyn
Truth Blooms Kelly Baker
Non-Verbal Learning Disorder Bree Rolfe
Love Staceyann Chin
Gender Se7en
No Homo Gazal Geoff Kagan Trenchard
I Hope You Know This Makes You a Fag Jude Bower
Fruit Adam Lowe
Talkin' with My Mother Gala Mukomolov
Gorgeous Disaster Amir Sulaiman
Finals Justin Long-Moton
The Salvation We Greet with Horror Jussi Jaakola
To Be Brought to Water Ricky Laurentiis
God Over Lunch Mike Ladd
2 Truths and a Lie Jennifer-Leigh Oprihory
Lunar Flora Sarah Martin
Science Says Erica Miriam Fabri
When It Matters Adam Falkner
Bayuk Rio Cortez
India Trio Sarah Kay
Ramadan Reflection Ainee Fatima
Woman Friend C. L. McFadyen
His Portable Pale Amber Reskey
It Could Be Words Taylor Mali

The Crow Flies Straight Quinn Patrick Kelly
Sidewalk Neighbor Taijhet Nyobi
Apuckerlipse Now Joan O' f(Art) (AKA Kali Liberick)
Of His Bones Are Coral Made Jacob Rakovan
Disclaimer/In Case of Emergency Don't Kwan Booth
The Rose Has Teeth Terrance Hayes
A Note Bent in Amber Peter Carlaftes
Wiping Up the Dance Floor in Alphabet City
Patricia Smith
Yolk Corey Zeller
A History of Violence April Jones
Air Max Barry Grass
My July Rachel Trignano
I'll Leave This Where You'll Find It Lauren Kaminski
Leeches C. Elliot
As I Enter the Night Etaïnn Zwer
Across the Street From the Whitmore
Home for Girls, 1949 Rachel McKibbens
Oh Ladies of the Light Shanita Bigelow
Rules of Engagement Jennifer Falu
End of Book Poem Jasper Faolan
Into Darkness Connor Pierce
The Whiskey Trail Glen Byford
GloryBox Didier Charlemagne
Breathe Slow My Parent Brett Bevell
Seated by the Well of Limpid Joys Sibylla Barthes
Scavenged Tongues and Buried Whispers Eden Jeffries
Kissing Caits Meissner
Something Beautiful Abiodun Oyewole
KinShip Queen Godis

July IV **Sharlie Messinger**
7 Moments Of Revolution **Kathleen McLeod**
Notes Of The Ghostlike **Bonafide Rojas**
Handstitch **Carlos Andrés Goméz**
A Trigger Down **Dominic Viti**
Breakfast in Blame **Emily Rose Larsen**
Transient **Joshua Kleinberg**
Connections **Matt Mason**
Mombasa **David Cairns**
Guerilla Garden Writing Poem **Inua Ellams**
Franklin Ave. & Anthony St., Newark **Tara Betts**
The Circadian Enigma **Ricky Ray**
Because **Ila Mira Kavanagh**
We Have the Right to **Vincent Toro**
Happiness **Victorio Reyes**
Sierra Nevada **Major Jackson**
Almost Certainly **Bohdan Piasecki**
The Poem in Red **Saul Williams**

Acknowledgments

Over the years, I have encountered thousands of poets who have handed me their work, asking me to read it, and in some cases, to find ways to help them get published. This book comes as a result of those daring, thoughtful, and important voices that I have encountered while wondering how I might share the opportunities afforded me, while also staying true to my own creative vision.

The idea of editing an anthology of modern, living poets was intriguing, but not intriguing enough, for one simple reason: I seldom read anthologies. Thus, the idea of creating a literary mixtape was born, where I made an attempt to weave poems and voices together as a DJ would, noting the tempo, mood, and theme of each piece and attempting to find a smooth way of blending into the next. Of course, it was no easy task and there is no way possible that I would have been able to complete the vision without a great deal of help. First I would like to thank the hundreds of poets who saw fit to respond to my call out through social media networks, to collaborate with me on an idea of questionable results. We made no mention of subject or theme and poets were free to submit two poems on any topic they chose. We received over 7,000 poems! Obviously, we couldn't place every poem in the book, but the intent remains for everyone to feel included as part of this *Chorus*. Your voices and work are crucial to my own, and to our times. I hope that you all see fit to continue expressing your visions, ideas, dissatisfaction, angst, and all that makes poetry serve as a vital essence of a culture. On my end, I was lucky enough to enlist the help and guidance of my two developmental editors, Aja Monet and Dufflyn Lammers. This book would not be possible if it were not for the long hours they spent reading through poems, offering suggestions, communicating with poets, and waiting for an often noncommunicative me to respond to their queries. Teamwork is truly the name of the game and I am lucky enough to be supported by a team of hardworking visionaries who don't say "yes" to my every idea, but certainly support the manifestation of many of my dreams. My literary agent, Charlotte Gusay, is as rock-and-roll as they come, with treasure troves of stories and ideas. I would like to thank her for all of the time, hard work, and belief she invested into this project (and those that came before). I sincerely hope that many of the poets included will one day be lucky enough to have a Charlotte Gusay on their team. My MTV Books editor, Jacob Hoye, is guilty by association and daring enough to have remained such an essential part of my literary efforts. Thanks, man. I'd also like to thank my enthusiastic editor, Ed Schlesinger, at Gallery/S&S who took over for Jennifer Heddle, and is as kind and open as she was. Thank you, also, to the staff of S&S for their hard work and participation, including Mary McCue, our publicist, and Steve Fallert in the Legal department.

Lastly, I would like to thank Sol Guy and Dave Guenette for their expertise, hard work, and vision. You'll be hearing more about them as we move forward. Finding the right team may take years to take shape, but when it does, watch out!

And, oh yeah, Fuck You, to whomever deserves it. You ain't shit, punk. #justsayin

Saulito Bonaparte
Paris 2012

Acclaimed poet and musician **Saul Williams**'s open-mic escapades with the Nuyorican Poets peaked at Sundance when *Slam* won the Grand Jury Prize, and the art world celebrated the arrival of a whole new kind of talent. He defied his genre's precious reputation and tore voraciously into the guts of life, groping after the exalted and transcendent sex sensations that make it all worth living. His early success led to collaborations with the likes of Erykah Badu, Nas, The Roots and Zack de la Rocha, and, descended as much from KRS-One and Public Enemy as Allen Ginsberg and Amiri Baraka, he was a new kind of poet. With each of Williams's great successes has come abrupt change. He has pinball-bounced from Morehouse philosophy scholar to cerebral street sermonizer to breakout indie actor, from hallucinatory hip-hop alchemist to dreadlocked mohawk rockstar, vibing Nine Inch Nails, scurrying across tones, modes, and media to defy categorization. He has read published poetry volumes to opera house audiences with full orchestral backing. He has contributed to the *New York Times*, voiced Jean-Michel Basquiat in *Downtown 81*, and cut records with Rick Rubin and Trent Reznor. Throughout all these chaotic ventures, Saul Williams has been one steady thing: an uncompromising voice determined to tap the adrenaline center of his existence with any tool he can get his hands on. Saul Williams is the author of four books of poetry. He lives in Paris. His website: www.saulwilliams.com

Poet, actor, journalist, **Dufflyn Lammers** has brought her unique style of "page-to-stage" poetry to universities from Smith College to UC Irvine, and is a fixture on the poetry and literary scene. She worked as Arts & Entertainment journalist for *The Georgia Guardian* and Morris News Service (from 1995 to 2000). Lammers was the host and Slam Master of the Los Feliz Poetry Slam at the Formosa Café in Hollywood and competed in the National Poetry Slam from 2000 through 2004. She has appeared in *Russell Simmons Def Poetry Jam* on HBO, in the film *Belly* from Artisan Films, and on ABC Television's *Eye on L.A.* She is the voice of the Baja Fresh "Spoken Word Radio" campaign and has appeared in episodes of *Criminal Minds, Entourage,* and more. She is anthologized in *Slam: The Competitive Art of Performance Poetry* (Manic D Press). Lammers lives in Los Angeles and is working on her first book—a memoir. For more go to: www.dufflyn.com

Poet and lyricist from East New York, Brooklyn, **Aja Monet**—at the age of nineteen—became the youngest individual to ever win the legendary Nuyorican Poet's Cafe Grand Slam champion title (2007). Monet received a BA from Sarah Lawrence College and an MFA in Creative Writing from the School of the Art Institute of Chicago. Aja Monet's poems have appeared in *The New York Times* and in numerous international television and radio programs. Her first book, *The Black Unicorn Sings,* was independently published with Penmanship Books. She is currently living in Paris and is working on a book of science fiction. To see her work, visit: www.ajamonet.com